# THE
# AMAZING
# TECHNICOLOUR
# PYJAMA
# THERAPY

# THE AMAZING TECHNICOLOUR PYJAMA THERAPY

## EMILY ACKERMAN

**Muddy**
Pearl

First published in 2014 by
Muddy Pearl, Edinburgh, Scotland.
www.muddypearl.com
books@muddypearl.com

*British Library Cataloguing in Publication Data*
A catalogue record for this book is available from the British Library

ISBN 978-1-910012-12-3

Typeset in Minion by Waverley Typesetters, Warham, Norfolk
Printed in Great Britain by Bell & Bain Ltd, Glasgow

*This book is dedicated to my amazing husband,*
*who loves through thick and thin.*

# CONTENTS

# FOREWORD

*'This book is all about fighting back. It's about reclaiming your life now you're ill, finding new ways to live well and serve effectively. You'll find survival strategies, encouragement, practical advice and fresh ways to view your situation.'*

With these striking words in the first chapter, Emily Ackerman accurately summarizes the purpose of her work. I could not find a better way to start this foreword because her words contain the main seeds she eventually sows in this moving book.

When our mutual friend, psychiatrist Rob Waller, asked me to write a foreword for *The Amazing Technicolour Pyjama Therapy*, I did not hesitate to respond affirmatively. I had two reasons to accept. First, although I have never met the author personally, I feel very near to Emily, as if we had known each other for years. It is that sort of mysterious closeness that she rightly calls 'the fellowship of suffering'; it is the nearness which arises from sharing the experience of the 'furnace of trial' or, in the author's own words, that 'strange and scary place people living with illness have in common'.

The second reason to accept was my conviction that this book will offer great comfort and practical help to those who are 'struck down but not destroyed', or I should rather say, to those who are actively struggling not to be destroyed. To put it in her own words: *'It took me a long time to learn that God was not out to kill me. Instead, he was offering me a new opportunity for growth and fruitfulness. He carefully provided everything I needed to survive and thrive in the face of pain and loss.'*

Emily writes with great moral authority because she has been – and she still is – in the furnace of trial. Notice her poignant words: *'Before I was ill I worked as a doctor. Now I'm a patient.'* This unusual combination of Biblical wisdom, professional skill as a former doctor and personal experience make this work a very helpful tool for those suffering from long term illness and their relatives.

As I read *The Amazing Technicolour Pyjama Therapy* I noticed that my spirit was slowly filled with an unexpected sense of joy and peace. I wondered why. By the end of the book, I had found out. It is a well-written book, I should say beautifully written, using a language that reflects both a tender heart and a lucid mind. It is also light reading and easy to digest, because Emily knows very well that sick people do not have a great deal of energy. These, however, were not the reasons that explained my unexpected sense of wellbeing. There is something deeper behind it: Emily invites us to join her in her own life trip through the desert of long illness. In this journey her point of reference is the abundant life Christ wants everybody to enjoy, regardless of their handicaps or severe thorns. She makes clear that our ultimate source of joy, meaning and happiness in life cannot be found apart from God. I am sure that this is the reason why, as you read this book, you are not likely to feel glad but you will indeed experience joy, the joy that comes from contemplating life with the eyes of the psalmist when he writes: 'You have made known to me the path of life; you will fill me with joy in your presence' (Psalm 16:11).

One last consideration from a more personal viewpoint. When I wrote *A Thorn in the Flesh: Finding strength and hope amid suffering* a few years ago I had one clear purpose in mind: 'to focus on the light of hope rather than on the darkness of the trial; to speak of victory rather than defeat; not to be paralysed by the thorn's venom but rather strengthened by the supernatural antidote of grace.'

This is exactly what Emily has achieved in her book. This is why I warmly recommend *The Amazing Technicolour Pyjama Therapy*. It will be like water in the desert, providing you with a refreshing perspective on illness and suffering.

DR. PABLO MARTINEZ, psychiatrist and author

# ACKNOWLEDGEMENTS

I'd like to sincerely thank all the people who have contributed to this book. Many of them are ill and exhausted, yet worked hard to offer me their wisdom. Thanks are also due to Dr Maureen Gowans, my pom-pom waving friends and my supportive and talented editor Stephanie Heald. My husband helpfully talked through much of the book content at the half-baked stage. Special thanks are due to my trusty green dressing gown, which clothed me during most of my writing sessions.

# MAKING A START

There's something about me you need to know, right at the start. My life's ambition is to be more like a spring onion.

My spring onions look small and weedy next to my neighbour's towering runner bean plants. But onions have a secret weapon. You can chop them off at the ankles and eat the shoots – and they don't die. They just shrug their wee roots and start all over again. Isn't that something?

*"There's just something about you that makes me think of spring onions."*

They don't despair, grumble or groan. They just crack on and grow like mad. Meanwhile, I get to eat the fresh green tops. What a useful plant.

To be fair, I am quite nice to my spring onions. They grow in a sunny spot in well-watered, carefully-nourished soil. If I just ignored them, they would give up and die.

When I fell ill and stayed ill, I felt like God had chopped me off at the ankles. I wasn't as brave as my onions, let me tell you. I yelped in pain and indignation; I felt painfully abandoned, diminished and finished.

It took me a long time to learn that God was not out to kill me. Instead, he was offering me a new opportunity for growth and fruitfulness. He carefully provided everything I needed to survive and thrive in the face of pain and loss. Over time I realised that I could fill up on the good things he was offering. I began to look my illness in the eye and fight back.

This book is all about fighting back. It's about reclaiming your life now you're ill, finding new ways to live well and serve effectively. You'll find survival strategies, encouragement, practical advice and fresh ways to view your situation. God hasn't given up on you; there's plenty of good news from the Bible about living abundantly and usefully with illness.[1]

There's a lot to think about and try out in this book. We're all different, so some ideas will suit you better than others. I wrote the book to be read from start to finish, but it is also good for dipping in and out of according to your energy and your interests.

## THE FELLOWSHIP OF SUFFERING

The sick are exiled into a strange and scary place, leaving behind great chunks of their previous way of life. It's a lonely transition, with pressures that well friends just can't understand.

---

[1] I'm writing from the perspective of a believing Christian. Throughout my illness, my faith has been more than a crutch, more than a stretcher. If you'd like to know more, you could check out www.christianity.org.uk, sign up for an Alpha course at your local church, or just start reading the Bible. Start at the Gospel of Mark and say a simple prayer – just ask God to show you more about himself as you read. If you'd like to know more about Christian faith, you could check out *www.christianity.org.uk.*

On the other hand, people living with illness have a lot in common. So, I thought, let's learn from one another. Over the years I've asked a lot of ill people a lot of questions. I've gleaned hard-won truths from folks with different illnesses, both physical and mental. Their experiences, faith and wisdom will keep us company along the way.

## Where I began

In my twenties, I happily juggled my career with a young family, hobbies, sport, friends and church life. My busy life was suddenly whipped from under my feet by a mystery illness. For many months I lay in bed in a state of shock, lost without the certainties of the past.

I cried out for God's power to relieve my suffering and allow me to fulfil my life plans. What I got was God's power changing me slowly through my struggles, so I could begin to fulfil *his* plans for my life. (Don't you hate it when God gives you what you need instead of what you want?)

Although I hadn't signed up for this particular adventure, I had, thinking back, rashly given my Lord the right to choose my path. I watched others zip ahead, choosing jobs, activities and lifestyle. I seemed to be left way behind, struggling with my situation day by day. Could this really be God's best for me?

Over a long and painful period I learned that although my path is unusual, I still have a life to live. I have choices, responsibilities and joys, like anybody else. And through my mistakes I slowly learned some nifty strategies to help me live well while I'm ill.

Before I was ill I worked as a doctor. Now I'm a patient. Ironic, eh? Although I had to leave my job, I found that being a doctor doesn't wash off. I still see things from that perspective. Through my work I met and tried to help many ill people. Now I understand a whole lot more about their point of view. So these days, I'm perched in the middle.

## Why Joseph?

I've been particularly drawn to the dramatic story of Joseph in the Bible during my long illness. Joseph's struggles seem to mirror the stages of life with illness. His strategies for handling trust, hope, pain, rejection and disempowerment are practical and useful. I'm encouraged that Joseph's destiny was not derailed by his troubles. The more I look, the more I find. So Joseph is our Bible companion as we consider life with illness.

If you don't know the story, here's a quick overview. We'll come back to reflect on different aspects throughout this book.

> *God spoke to young Joseph in two dreams, which foretold high leadership responsibilities. His jealous older brothers then sold Joseph to slave traders to get rid of him. He was taken to Egypt and sold on to became a manager in Potiphar's house. Potiphar's wife tried to seduce Joseph but when he refused, she successfully framed him for rape.*
>
> *Joseph was imprisoned for several years and became the prison manager. Two of Pharaoh's servants were held in the same prison. Both of them had troubling dreams which Joseph accurately interpreted. Later, Pharaoh had significant dreams of his own and Joseph interpreted these as a warning of widespread crop failure. Pharaoh was impressed by Joseph and put him in charge of a huge famine relief programme.*
>
> *When Joseph's brothers came to Egypt to buy food from Joseph, he recognised them although they didn't realise who he was. He tested their motives before revealing the truth. The brothers then went home to get their families and returned to live securely in Egypt.*
>
> *Joseph's God-given managerial skills and serving attitude saved millions of people from starvation, including his own family. God's calling over Joseph's life came dramatically true after many years of suffering and hardship.*

Joseph's adventures begin in Genesis 37:1. I'll give the references as we go. If you have the energy, it's a good idea to read the Bible passages alongside this book.

## DREAMS AND DESTINY

GENESIS 37:1–11

Joseph dreamed his famous dreams as a privileged teenager, living comfortably in a large family. At that time, people in the area viewed dreams and their interpretation as important business. Skilled practitioners wrote dream texts with detailed lists of symbols and meanings. Some of these fragile scrolls have survived to this day, because they were carefully preserved as treasured possessions. So it was natural for Joseph to take his dreams seriously, as a sign of his future.

Joseph's dreams didn't arrive on any random night. God had a detailed plan that stretched over many years. He knew that Joseph would need time to develop in skills and integrity. God set out Joseph's timetable perfectly so that Joseph would be ready for his big chance.

God has the same kind of loving, purposeful oversight over every human life. We weren't created to be ignored or wasted but to live out God's good plans for us. Our limited viewpoint is a huge drawback in hard times. Like Joseph, we must live through the pain without seeing the end point, trying to hang on to God's promises as we go.

### A false step

Recognising God's call is only the beginning. Joseph reacted by boasting immaturely to his older brothers;

> Joseph had a dream, and when he told it to his brothers, they hated him all the more. He said to them, 'Listen to this dream I had: We were binding sheaves of corn out in the field when suddenly my sheaf rose and stood upright, while your sheaves gathered around mine and bowed down to it.'
>
> His brothers said to him, 'Do you intend to reign over us? Will you actually rule us?' And they hated him all the more because of his dream and what he had said.

GENESIS 37:5–8

Oh dear. Joseph hit trouble because he tried to use his calling to make himself look big. He still had a lot to learn.

### Another kind of dream

God spoke to Joseph powerfully, using Joseph's night-time dreams. There's a different kind of dream that also fuels human ambition and purpose. Life dreams, our long-held, treasured plans, are vital to preserving vision and hope.

Life dreams have had a hard time lately, hijacked and devalued by Western culture. Consumer goods like cars and long-haul holidays have been promoted as life dreams. Something you can buy is no replacement for a passionate personal vision to build a better world. A genuine life dream is a true gift from God.

When my illness hit, I felt as if my precious life dreams were ripped away. I longed to support broken people and express my creativity but I couldn't even get out of bed. I watched sadly as others lived their lives to the full. Over time, my hope and confidence quietly wilted and died.

It eased my sorrow when I grasped the difference between gifts and life dreams. Gifts are the permanent package of strengths and passions that God gives each person before birth. Life dreams spring from underlying gifts and are shaped by culture, family, education and experience. As we go through life we discover our gifts and many of us find a life dream, or dreams, which tend to be more specific.

So young Joseph had the gifts of administration and leadership from birth, which made him a very effective farm worker. His life dream of great leadership was sparked by his God-given sleeping dreams. Others find their life dreams through prayer, quiet reflection or the encouragement of a wise observer. If you find yourself consistently drawn to something good, angered by an injustice or can't ignore the needs of a particular group, this may be the area of your life dream.

### A bigger dream

Our life dreams are based on what we know and imagine now. Even if we've grasped God's call, our reactions to that call are often a bit naïve or self-centred. Like Joseph, I've been guilty of trying to use my calling to give me significance. God meanwhile waits patiently for me to get the point. His love is there to build me up, while his calling over my life is a gift of love from him to others.

*'For I know the plans I have for you,'* declares the LORD, *'plans to prosper you and not to harm you, plans to give you hope and a future.'*

JEREMIAH 29:11

This beautiful promise was given to the people of Israel at a very low point in their history. It shows that in spite of the messy bits, God's perspective on our small lives is eternal, wise and wonderful. When our human hopes and dreams fall away, they leave space for something new. God has powerful plans for us that are far beyond anything we can imagine. Our gifts are still safely in place.

If this idea seems way out of reach right now, maybe it's not time yet. After diagnosis, the first priority is to survive day by day, to grasp a new reality and start to let go of the past. That's a big step for anyone to master. As the grief and shock wear off, we'll come round to look at this again.

## *For reflection*

**1** Think of somebody you know who's sick or suffering. Have you learned anything useful from them?

**2** What were your childhood dreams? Are they still the same today? Could you ask God to show you if all these dreams are from him?

**3** Which barriers stand in the way of your dreams? Imagine the barriers as big rocks blocking your path. Now picture the Holy Spirit flowing like a river. See how the water always finds a way around, under or past the rocks, or washes them away over time. Ask God to make a path for you so your journey can continue, despite what's in your way.

*Affliction is able to drown out every earthly voice . . . but the voice of eternity within a man it cannot drown*

SOREN KIERKEGAARD, *Christian Discourses*

*God be in my head and in my understanding;*
*God be in my eyes and in my looking;*
*God be in my mouth and in my speaking;*
*God be in my heart and in my thinking;*
*God be at my end and in my departing.*

OLD SARUM PRAYER, FIRST RECORDED 1514

*I'm sick of following my dreams. I'm just going to ask them*
*where they're going, and hook up with them later.*

MITCH HEDBERG

# IN THE PIT

2

*So Joseph went after his brothers and found them near Dothan.
But they saw him in the distance, and before he reached them,
they plotted to kill him.*

*'Here comes that dreamer!' they said to each other. 'Come
now, let's kill him and throw him into one of these cisterns and
say that a ferocious animal devoured him. Then we'll see what
comes of his dreams.'*

GENESIS 37:17b–20

After those wonderful dreams, the next stage in Joseph's life was starkly painful. His cosy way of life was stripped away when he went from running an errand to fighting for his life. When his brothers ripped the special robe from his back, he lost his identity as a favourite son. Even worse, landing in a waterless pit in the desert meant death was not far away. Joseph was helpless, in danger and alone.

I once did a Sunday school session on Joseph in the pit. We invited the children to write down what Joseph might have prayed. My favourite contribution ran, '*Lord, get me out of this pit NOW or I'll never go to church again!*'

Of course Joseph asked God for deliverance. Perhaps he also bargained, cried, pleaded and shouted his outrage from down there in the dust. After all, God had promised him a bright future. Surely this was just a diversion and he would soon be back on track.

### Why was God silent?

God surely heard Joseph's prayers. But Joseph's destiny and God's plan could only be worked out by leaving Joseph right there. Joseph was God's man for the job but he lacked experience, people skills, maturity and faith. The struggles to come were needed to prepare him for success.

And so instead of rescue, God gave Joseph the prickly gifts of suffering and loss.

Even as Joseph licked dry lips in that horrible hole, God was looking into the future with love. If God had rescued him that day, millions of people would later have starved, including Joseph and his family.

Of course, Joseph lacked this eternal perspective. He could only despair, or choose to trust God for what he couldn't understand.

## FALLING ILL

Joseph isn't alone down there, because we all end up in a pit at some point. Let's peep over the edge of the illness pit and see what's at the bottom.

Some illnesses begin with a bang, whipped off to hospital or flattened into bed. Other conditions creep in until normal life is no longer normal. Either way, it's a very difficult transition. Previous life skills are suddenly out of date. We find out how much we've relied on our comfort zones. When work, socialising and hobbies are out of reach, it's a new and scary world.

It seems there's no time to adjust. There are new challenges to face, starting with unwelcome and frightening symptoms. There's the shock of getting a diagnosis, or the fight to find out what's wrong. There are harsh new limits and perhaps open-ended time off work or study. Financial pressure also forces unwanted change.

Then there are personal changes to figure out, like finding some friends have gone silent. We may feel that we've lost part of ourselves.

At the time it seems like a killer blow. Newly ill people naturally strive to get back to where they were. That boring old life looks wonderful now it's out of reach. The grieving process starts to kick in as we realise that the old is gone. We may recover, but we won't be the same.

This painful moment of truth leads on to renewed hope. Nobody's life stands still forever. Yes, things are changing – but with God's help, some things can change for the better.

## Diagnosis

What was it like when you were diagnosed? Do you remember, or was it way back in childhood?[2] Maybe you felt shocked, frightened or full of questions.

For James, a long history of psychological and social difficulties was crowned by a diagnosis of schizophrenia. He found that loss of identity struck deep:

> *Suddenly I was a schizophrenic. Nothing that I'd accomplished with my life seemed relevant any more. Why label me by my illness? Nobody calls someone a broken leg.*

It's almost as if James lost the right to be a person. He was admitted to hospital without a choice, too ill to think straight. James was poorly, in need of care and sanctuary, but not so ill that he couldn't spot the downside.

The moment of diagnosis can be mind-blowing. Neil was told he had advanced bladder cancer:

> *The oncologist told us bluntly that I had T3 cancer, needed to have my damaged bladder out, and that he was the most experienced plumber in the country.*
>
> *The next ten minutes were a careful explanation of all possible treatments, but as it was all quite new, I didn't have enough bandwidth to download it all. I just kept imagining having an external bladder, and how I would rock climb, carry sacks of coal and plane timber without leaking.*

It's no wonder he felt dazed and daunted, faced with big choices at such a vulnerable moment.

### But what's the matter?

Sometimes it feels like any diagnosis is better than no diagnosis. I had five scary months of feeling horrible, running a high fever and unable to think clearly or walk straight. Meanwhile my GP commented on how well I looked and reluctantly ordered tests that came back normal. My family

---

[2] Chapter 16 looks at the impact of illnesses that start in childhood.

and friends naturally wanted a diagnosis they could understand. I was left hoping they would continue to believe me.

Finally I crawled pale-faced into work, just to show willing. A passing doctor diagnosed me with ME on the spot. When the diagnosis was confirmed I felt nothing but relief. At last I had an answer; at least I wasn't dying there and then.

So for some, diagnosis brings relief from uncertainty and a chance to move forward with treatment. For others, it's a shock – the worst thing possible, or an illness they'd never even heard of. The attitude of those who break the news is really important, making a memory that remains.

## FACING THE GRIEF

Sunil had a car accident that left him with severe back problems:

> In the early days I felt severely deprived of life. I didn't know if I could go back to work. It was hard to accept laying down my church activities: youth, music, worship leading etc. The sense of loss was acute.

Sunil suddenly hit strict limitations, painful symptoms and major lifestyle changes. It's no wonder he struggled with his feelings.

Sunil had to grieve for his previous self and the details of his previous life; playing in a band, active days spent out of doors, DIY projects and youth camps. Meanwhile those around him were grieving too. This grieving process takes many newly-ill people by surprise.

Grief will pass, if it's allowed out, and the initial shock also clears over time. At the same time Sunil was learning how to manage his illness and how to approach this new challenge. Over time he recovered emotionally, regaining confidence and the ability to think practically. The illness alone was less daunting without the early feelings on top.

### Good grief

Grief is the way humans process rapid change and loss. It involves intense feelings and unusual reactions like numbness, denial, pain, sadness, anger, guilt, shame, confusion and bargaining. Mood swings, vivid memories of the past, irritability, tearfulness, exhaustion and poor concentration are normal. For a time, ordinary life is set aside.

After the first flood of grief settles, fresh waves of grief are triggered by reminders of loss. These waves will recede faster if the pain is expressed. This stage makes me think of standing on the shore as the tide goes out. I may get soaked by each wave but I'm no longer floating helplessly in a stormy sea.

A period of reflection takes up a lot of time and effort, triggering deep questions: Why has this happened to me? Did I bring this on myself? Does God still love me?

This is an important time of growth and adjustment, even though it hurts. Trying to snap out of it won't help. Illness is a major life event and deserves some attention.

### A safe space

So allowing time to work through grief and shock is essential. Grief is meant to be a journey, not a destination. Denying difficult feelings is tempting but it just creates a bigger burden up ahead. Fresh grief is bad enough; stale grief is toxic.

Letting my feelings out can put pressure on relationships, particularly if I'm angry today. I find it helps to write, weep, draw or speak out my thoughts when I'm alone. It also helps to talk to someone safe, like a friend, patient help-line, minister or counsellor.

Of course, I can talk to God at any time. Although he knows my situation, it makes a huge difference to me to talk it through with him.

Christians sometimes try to 'tidy up' before praying, or just avoid God altogether when things are bad. But those amazing Bible heroes show me that it's fine to bring my messy self to God for his help and comfort. Here's a heartfelt prayer from mighty King David himself:

> To you, LORD, I call;
> you are my Rock,
> do not turn a deaf ear to me.
> For if you remain silent,
> I shall be like those who go down to the pit.
> Hear my cry for mercy
> as I call to you for help,

> *as I lift up my hands*
> *towards your Most Holy Place.*

PSALM 28:1–2

This anguished cry for help reminds me of my neighbour Jen's famous cat, who got run over at the end of the street one day. The poor cat lost half of its tail and one back leg was completely severed. Fighting off all help, the cat picked up its leg in its mouth and set off for home, trailing blood and yowling with pain. It limped to the open communal door and somehow climbed two flights of stairs before collapsing on Jen's doormat, where she found it after work. She scooped up mat, cat, leg and all and

*"And another thing you don't seem to realise ..."*

rushed it to the vet for emergency surgery. The cat recovered to live a long and adventurous three-legged life. It survived because it knew that when trouble hits, it's best to take your pain to someone who cares.

Early on, I used to pray at night by mentally composing letters to God. They tended to start like this; 'Dear Sir, it recently has come to my attention that despite a binding contract *in writing* of your endless love, compassion and provision (see list of references below), you've seen fit to land me in deep doo-doo,[3] turn your back and walk away.' Out poured all my pain, rage, fear and confusion. Out came all the bitter complaints and accusations against God's Word and character. I knew this wasn't a respectful way to address God. I also knew that if I didn't let out my feelings I would hit someone hard, or have a breakdown. It seemed better to me to keep talking to God, even if I couldn't find anything nice to say. So I suppose I was copying the cat by carrying my pain to God's door. And like the cat, I didn't know what to do when I got there.

My brutal honesty had its place. God is big enough to cope with my yowling and I kept in touch with God rather than withdrawing altogether. It was better than splurging my daily pain, rage and fear over my suffering family. Eventually I was able to work through the pain to reach a better perspective. I'm not alone. The Psalms include many undignified yells of fear and outrage:

> I am overwhelmed with troubles
>   and my life draws near to death.
> I am counted among those who go down to the pit;
>   I am like one without strength.
> I am set apart with the dead,
>   like the slain who lie in the grave,
> whom you remember no more,
>   who are cut off from your care . . .
>
> But I cry to you for help, LORD;
>   in the morning my prayer comes before you.
> Why, LORD, do you reject me
>   and hide your face from me?

PSALM 88:3–5 and 13–14

---

[3] To be absolutely honest, my actual language was a little more colourful than this.

### No need to rush

Everybody longs for these feelings to go away, but there's no prize for 'first past the post'. Facing the pain takes courage and energy and happens at its own pace. There's a healthy balance between the two pitfalls of denial and dwelling endlessly on loss. I find that sometimes it's right to make room for reflection and sometimes it's better to distract myself. As grief starts to resolve, the feelings fade and the endless questions start to rephrase themselves into more useful forms.

After diagnosis we may wonder exactly what we will lose. It takes time for things to settle, to see if that career break will be permanent, or perhaps health will improve with treatment. So grieving happens in stages as we realise which doors have closed. We'll come back to this idea later in the book.

## TRUE LOVE

Geeta broke several bones in a car accident. Coming round after emergency surgery, she resolved that if she prayed, she wouldn't need any pain relief because God would surely look after her. When she was literally forced to ask for medication, she was also forced to reconsider her view of God's loving provision for her life. At that moment, Geeta was in her personal pit.

When I was in my 'newly ill' pit, I too found myself painfully revisiting my ideas. My immature beliefs were holding me back from receiving God's blessings. Here's the kind of thing I mean:

* God loves me, so I will always be safe, well and content.
* God loves me, so if something bad happens, he will always rescue me.
* God heals today, so he will heal me whenever I'm sick.

I discovered, along with Geeta, that God is not a vending machine, poised to serve up what I want, when I want it. His ways are not our ways. Despite this, his love is personal, true, lasting and dependable.

### God knows my name

GENESIS 37:25–6

Back at that long-ago desert pit, God's loving plans for Joseph contrast sharply with the attitudes of Joseph's family. What a horrible bunch. Joseph's brothers sold him to their own second cousins, who were slave traders. At every step it was hammered home that Joseph had lost his place as a favoured son of the tribe. He was reduced to slavery, nameless and alone, a product to be traded. According to the customs of the time, he was 'trademarked' – tattooed or branded – and he knew he would be sold on to the highest bidder.

Slavery continues to this day; this is a great evil that's worth fighting. When it comes to illness, Joseph's suffering reminds me that loss of health is a huge disadvantage in our results-driven culture. Loss of face is one thing, but what about becoming faceless? Voiceless?

## Who am I?

It's as if the well world puts sick people into a box, slams the lid and slaps a label across the top.

Labels carry a simple message. Once they're on, they stick like mad and are hard to get off again. Sometimes we join in and label ourselves. Here are some labels stuck to the sick, whether spoken or unspoken:

> *Victim, Patient, Mad, Hypochondriac, Lazy, Different, Poor Soul, Wonderful, Disabled, Weird, Unemployed, Housebound, Invalid, Ill.*

These words boil down to two basic themes: different and sub-standard. Labels don't show the complexity of real life. They cut us off from others and keep us stuck where we are.

Looking more closely at identity, the next level is the roles we play:

> *Wife, Son, Employee, Boss, Clown, Scatty blonde, Friend, Victim, Helper, Sports fan and so on.*

These words are about what we do and how we fit in. We like to know our place, so when the roles fall away we're left bereft. Roles express more than labels but still fail to reach the heart.

God takes a far more radical approach to human identity. His perspective is deep and searching, looking back to our beginnings, sweeping through this moment and forwards to our eternal destiny. Joseph's name means 'God will increase.' Joseph's destiny, his role, was built into him, as part of his identity, like a brightly coloured thread woven through a length of cloth. God had chosen him to deliver millions of people from starvation. First he called him, and then lovingly trained and helped Joseph to prepare him for the job. God appointed Joseph to be part of the family business, the Kingdom of God, just as he appoints us. Each person has his or her own God-ordained destiny. God's call begins and shapes a lifelong individual journey.

Becoming a doctor works the other way around. First, I trained and sacrificed for long hard years. I wondered if I would ever make it. Then on my first day at work I was issued with a hospital identity badge that said 'Dr Emily Ackerman'. Oh, I was proud of that hard-earned badge. But God starts by giving me my badge, identifying my unique destiny, even though I don't understand all the details. After that, my training begins. That's why a call from God is often followed by setbacks and challenges. My identity and calling remain secure; I already have my place.

### My Heavenly pet name

Of course God knows my name, the one I use day by day – but there's more. The Bible shows how God tenderly shows his love to us by giving us names. These pet names, endearments or titles reflect a believer's relationship with the Father and describe our high calling in this world and the next. Here are a few:

| | | |
|---|---|---|
| *Beloved* | *Believer* | *Saint* |
| *Mine* | *Holy* | *Disciple* |
| *Chosen* | *Redeemed* | *Accepted* |
| *Heir* | *Royal priesthood* | |
| *Son or daughter* | *Servant* | |

When I feel diminished because of illness and loss, the perfect antidote is found right here. This is the truth running deep through my life, far beyond the reach of any label or snap judgement. First and foremost, I belong to a loving God.

## *For Reflection*

**1** Are you grieving for your old life? How does this affect you?

**2** Do you think it's acceptable for a Christian to express sadness to God? How about fear, confusion or anger? Is there a better place to consider these feelings?

**3** Do you think you've been labelled by others, or yourself, since you fell ill? Are the labels accurate?

**4** To start rebuilding your identity, pick one of God's pet names for you from the list given. Write it out with your own name included, like this –

'Emily is God's Beloved'
'Simon is Chosen'
'Lisa is a Disciple'

Now stick it up somewhere you will see it frequently. Read it out to yourself every day until it sinks in.

**5** Read Psalm 13

> *How long, LORD? Will you forget me forever?*
> *How long will you hide your face from me?*
> *How long must I wrestle with my thoughts*
> *and day after day have sorrow in my heart?*
> *How long will my enemy triumph over me?*
>
> *Look on me and answer, LORD my God.*
> *Give light to my eyes, or I will sleep in death,*
> *and my enemy will say, 'I have overcome him,'*
> *and my foes will rejoice when I fall.*
>
> *But I trust in your unfailing love;*
> *my heart rejoices in your salvation.*
> *I will sing the LORD's praise,*
> *for he has been good to me.*

Why do you think this passage is included in the Bible?

*Give sorrow words; the grief that does not speak whispers the o'er-fraught heart and bids it break*

**WILLIAM SHAKESPEARE**

*Though he brings grief, he will show compassion, so great is his unfailing love. For he does not willingly bring affliction or grief to anyone.*

**LAMENTATIONS 3:32–33**

*If you're going through hell, keep going*

WINSTON CHURCHILL

*Now the green blade riseth from the buried grain,*
*Wheat that in dark earth many days has lain;*
*Love lives again, that with the dead has been:*
*Love is come again, like wheat that springeth green.*

*In the grave they laid him, love whom men had slain,*
*Thinking that never he would wake again.*
*Laid in the earth like grain that sleeps unseen:*
*Love is come again, like wheat that springeth green,*

*Forth he came at Easter, like the risen grain,*
*He that for three days in the grave had lain.*
*Quick from the dead my risen Lord is seen:*
*Love is come again, like wheat that springeth green.*

*When our hearts are wintry, grieving, or in pain,*
*Thy touch can call us back to life again;*
*Fields of our hearts that dead and bare have been:*
*Love is come again, like wheat that springeth green.*

JOHN M. C. CRUM, *Oxford Book of Carols,* 1928

# HITTING YOUR STRIDE

## A NEW LIFE BEGINS

### GENESIS 39:1–6

Joseph was sold into slavery in far-off Egypt, serving in Potiphar's wealthy household. Joseph could have decided that since he didn't want to be there, he would sulk and skive. Instead, he chose to work hard and learn all he could.

For me, learning to live as a newly-sick person felt like being exiled to a harsh new country. Everything was strange and hard at first. Like Joseph, I'm still under God's care. I'm free to learn and free to choose my attitude every day, even when I choose badly.

The next section of the book looks at living successfully in this new country. Whatever's the matter with you, there are things that can help you get through the day. This chapter kicks off with pacing, offering a practical approach to your daily routine.

## PACING

Pacing yourself might seem a bit lazy. Westerners tend to live in a culture of achievement. The church often gets sucked in, urging members with high workloads to take on even more. We may believe that it's un-Christian to say no to others. Then Greek philosophy has given us the idea that spiritual welfare is way above the needs of mind and body. No wonder so many Christians are exhausted.

The Bible reveals God's way, right at the beginning of the world:

*By the seventh day God had finished the work he had been doing; so on the seventh day he rested from all his work.*

> *Then God blessed the seventh day and made it holy, because on*
> *it he rested from all the work of creating that he had done.*

GENESIS 2:2–3

God made the universe and then paused to reflect on what he had made. His work was meaningful and his rest was holy and blessed. Human beings are made in his image, so this rhythm of work and rest is important for us too.

A later passage takes this point a step further, starting with the people of Israel in the desert:

> *So, as the Holy Spirit says:*
> *'Today, if you hear his voice,*
> *do not harden your hearts*
> *as you did in the rebellion,*
> *during the time of testing in the wilderness,*
> *where your ancestors tested and tried me,*
> *though for forty years they saw what I did.*
> *That is why I was angry with that generation;*
> *I said, "Their hearts are always going astray,*
> *and they have not known my ways."*
> *So I declared on oath in my anger,*
> *"They shall never enter my rest."'*
> . . .
> *There remains, then, a Sabbath-rest for the people of God; for*
> *anyone who enters God's rest also rests from their works, just*
> *as God did from his.*
> *Let us, therefore, make every effort to enter that rest, so that*
> *no one will perish by following their example of disobedience.*

HEBREWS 3:7–11 and 4:9–11

So if we can't rest, it can be a sign that we're disobeying God, like the rebellious generation who never reached the Promised Land. It seems our rest is important to God. The effects of this disobedience are painfully obvious for the sick. I can work till I crash and deal with the consequences, or take my planned rest and carry on refreshed.

Many sick people are unable to work in the traditional sense. If that's you, perhaps you could look on managing your illness as useful work. Pacing is a good place to begin.

### Can pacing help me?

Pacing means building a realistic rhythm of work and rest. Every ill person who's able and willing can benefit from good pacing. If you recover, it will still be helpful to know how to balance your life. If you know recovery is unlikely and perhaps your time is short, pacing can help you to make the most of every day.

It works like running a budget. Let's say Jo has a low income, 37p in her bank account and no overdraft facility. Her life will go more smoothly if she faces reality, finds out how much she has for each day and lives within her means. If she gets it right, she'll have three meals and enough for bus fares to work the next day. Getting it wrong means new shoes and no dinner.

The sick have tight energy budgets and so we must learn to make the most of what we have, like Jo with her money. Leaving a little energy over for healing is like starting to save. Even a tiny sum each day will add up to a useful resource. On the other hand, forcing yourself to overdo is like taking out a pay-day loan. It has to be paid back later, plus the interest rate is crippling.

### I don't want to!

I appreciate the benefits of pacing now. But to begin with, I didn't like the look of it. Since there was no other treatment on offer, I had to get cracking. This is where things got interesting. I've learned a lot about myself through persevering with pacing.

First off, I resisted the idea of pacing because I didn't want to dwell on my illness. I decided to approach it as a short training course. After the initial habit-forming phase, I didn't have to think about it so much. These days I get more done, feel less stressed and rarely hit a crash-and-burn day.

Next, facing reality is an important part of the pacing process. It often feels easier to deny my state of health, to ignore the day's limits and just get on. The trouble with this is that denial stops me from living my life as it really is. Have a look at Chapter 7 for more about defeating denial.

Good pacing means caring for myself instead of running around after everybody else. As I tend to be a rescuer, I've had to work hard on this area. It seems to me now that a lot of my 'selfless' activity was compulsive caring. I was driven by my own poor boundaries, low self-esteem, fear of rejection and a flourishing Messiah complex. When I allowed others to dump their responsibilities onto me, or tried to lead their lives for them, I wasn't helping. In fact I was getting in God's way. Working through these issues has freed me to take care of myself and to serve others from a healthier perspective.

### Daily rhythms

Identifying your personal rhythms offers new possibilities. Think of a surfer who waits patiently to catch the wave, to avoid wasting effort and risking injury.

Each person has a range of abilities, each with its own rhythm: 'There is a time for everything, and a season for every activity under the heavens' (Ecclesiastes 3:1). If there's a time for every activity, there's also a less suitable time. Getting a grip on this concept releases fresh strength for living and healing.

To identify your own personal daily, weekly and female four-weekly rhythms, try keeping a diary or a time sheet. Put in what you did and when, and how you felt. If you're too poorly to do this, lie in bed and think carefully about the last week or so. This part needs extra energy for a few days. If you can't think straight or keep notes, perhaps someone could help. Looking back over this information will equip you to spot daily patterns. Look for waves of mental, emotional, physical and social energy. Don't forget the other side; note your energy slumps and symptom surges. With this information, it's possible to catch the wave by matching daily tasks to personal rhythms.

### Starting to change

Here's how it works for me. I do better all day if I have a slow start in the morning. Getting hungry, time-pressured or chilly has a really bad effect on me, so I plan my day to avoid these extremes. My head is usually clear in the late morning, so I write or do admin then. Napping before four in the afternoon means I can have my rest without damaging sleep at night. Later on in the day I get going physically, so I try to plan outings or activities for the early evening. I have a short-lived surge of energy after meals, too. Knowing and using these rhythms releases me to get more done without damage. The next stage is weekly patterns. I keep an eye on my diary to avoid over-busy days. I try to keep one day a week free, either for extra rest or unexpected activities. Here are a few tips for good pacing:

* Rest between activities.
* Avoid zig-zags, where a good day is followed by a crash day, and then after resting you get another good day and overdo again. Zig-zags are emotionally exhausting and delay recovery. Aim for an even keel.
* Avoid multi-tasking.
* Use a timer to avoid getting sucked in to activities like chatting on the phone or using a computer. I have one ticking right now.

Layla has cerebral palsy and other major illnesses to contend with. Here she describes her pacing strategies:

*These days I'm not afraid to ask for help, or to take it when it's offered. I have a morning care session, giving me energy for appointments and phone calls. Some days I still won't have energy for these things but it's better if I have the care.*

*Scheduling in regular rests helps, although I still feel guilty for resting. I trust my instincts about when to say no, and when to push myself and then deal with the fallout after.*

*I try to have two regular rest days in the week. My OT has warned me about my week being too busy on Monday and Tuesday, so I'm working on changing that.*

### Signpost symptoms

It's sometimes possible to use a particular symptom or visible change as a sign that it's time to rest. This is really handy if your illness pays you back later for overdoing, when it's too late to stop.

The actual symptom might be mild, so you really need to take notice. A carer or housemate may be well placed to help you with this 'spot the symptom' process. Your patient association might help, too. I learned that a common ME signpost is going pale round the mouth and this has proved very useful indeed.

James has schizophrenia. He lives alone and his illness can affect his insight. This signpost strategy helps James to assess his well being and ask for help at the right time.

His psychiatric nurse helped him to make a personalised list of signpost symptoms; his best early warning sign is disturbed sleep. James pinned up his list on the kitchen wall and looks at it often to see how he's doing.

## ONCE IN A WHILE

Big events and outings call for another level of pacing. I usually need to check access, food, timing and transport beforehand. Choosing and trying on my outfit ahead of time is fun, as I rarely get to dress up. It also saves last minute panic when the buttons no longer meet in the middle.

I find this pre-planned approach releases me to enjoy the best bits and let go of the rest. I have time to choose and negotiate what I can manage. This spares me from unrealistic expectations on the day.

A new holiday location may need careful research. Then there's organising what to pack. You could see it as a chore or relax and enjoy the run-up to your break. Getting organised in good time allows for a few days of extra rest before you tackle the journey.

You don't need to go far to enjoy a change of scene, particularly if you're too poorly to go out. I once had a very enjoyable mini-break in the home of friends who live less than a mile away.

### Left behind

What about when you can't attend? Making it clear that you're too ill and you're sad to miss out should help to soothe ruffled feathers. Perhaps seeing photos would make you feel included, or a plate of party food could be kept for you, along with someone's ticket or the order of service. If it's a funeral, you could light a candle, look at photos and remember the person and their impact on your life.

It's painful to be left out, particularly if the event is a happy one. Even something simple like a family day out can trigger feelings of loss, as others go where I cannot. It's normal to feel sad at these times.

### Oh, no, it's Christmas

Christmas used to suck up all my nerve and energy. These days I start early, spread out the work and have more energy left over for any last-minute fun on offer. Christmas isn't going to be cancelled. It's quite safe to plan ahead.

*"I'm sure you'll have fun at home too. I'll bring you a sausage roll and a party popper back."*

I put a Christmas carol CD on when I wrap gifts or write cards, even if it's October. Christmas Bible readings and Advent candles or calendars emphasise the season rather than one day. Organising small gifts for those around me is satisfying, adding me in to their celebrations. Choosing fair trade gifts, or making my own, adds to the sense of being useful in the world. If I can't get to church, CDs or the radio let me enjoy seasonal music.

Simone is often less well in winter, which affects both birthday and Christmas fun. She saves energy by welcoming visitors and saving the presents to open later. Organising visitors to come on different days lets her rest in between.

Christmas Day is a huge deal in our culture. If things aren't good, or you're alone, it can be a difficult day. It doesn't have to be like it is in the magazines. We're nudged towards having high expectations to stimulate profit for big business. Eating pasta in your pyjamas on Christmas Day could be seen as a radical anti-capitalist statement.

It helps me to dig deep into the Christmas story. It wasn't all cute babies, sparkly angels and fluffy lambs. The Gospel accounts tell a story of destiny, pain, steadfast love, courage, adventure, cruelty and a close shave with Roman soldiers. This is the real thing, God's gift of love to a broken world, the genuine magic of Christmas. I'd rather rest on the truth than wrap tinsel around my pain to impress the neighbours.

### Making a move

Many people feel the loss when they move house. A sick person who spends a lot of time at home may feel he is losing part of himself. If the move is forced by illness, as mine was, there's another layer of feelings to handle. Recognising these feelings releases extra energy to deal with the practicalities.

A successful move is made up of masses of small details. Keeping notes helps to tame the beast. I decided to collect the details and have a short 'moving admin' session every day. This approach relieved my dodgy memory, got results and conserved both energy and peace of mind.

On moving day, I stayed in bed till they came to put it in the van, the very last thing to go. A waist bag containing pills, keys, cash, mobile and a blow-up pillow kept me more or less together through the day. There was so much to do that I didn't have time to think about leaving my old home for the last time. Our new flat needed major renovation, which stirred up dust and mould. Fresh paint, dry rot treatments and new floor coverings gave off fumes for weeks. All of these are toxic, particularly if you're sick and stuck inside like me. We got most of the work done and dusted before the move, which helped a lot. A summer move-in date allowed us to air the property thoroughly without freezing the occupants.

It takes most people many months to settle in and find new places for all their bits and bobs. I found it paid to have low expectations. Creating a cosy corner offers a safe haven when the mess gets on top of you. If you keep writing down what's needed, you'll know what to say if someone offers to help. And if all else fails, close your eyes!

## STUMBLING BLOCK OR STEPPING-STONE?

Working on small daily habits may seem too slow, too tiny a response in the face of urgent suffering. I'd rather have a drastic cure to catapult me back to full health. It's all so frustrating.

The apostle Paul had his own frustrating problem. He kept asking God to remove it but God had other ideas:

> *Therefore, in order to keep me from becoming conceited, I was given a thorn in my flesh, a messenger of Satan, to torment me. Three times I pleaded with the Lord to take it away from me. But he said to me, 'My grace is sufficient for you, for my power is made perfect in weakness.' Therefore I will boast all the more gladly about my weaknesses, so that Christ's power may rest on me.*

2 CORINTHIANS 12:7b–9

This challenging passage offers two encouraging points. Firstly, Paul's difficulty persisted despite much prayer, great faith, sacrificial ministry and a close relationship with God. This helps me to stop worrying that I'm not good enough for healing, as if God would be so petty.

31

Next, there was a good reason for Paul's suffering. God wanted to do more through Paul, whose self-sufficiency was getting in the way. God's plan was to increase Paul's fruitfulness by building reserves of humility and trust. Looking back, Paul understood that this difficulty had made him a more effective evangelist and a better man.

I've found it hard to face this passage when things are tough. But these principles offer valid hope and a sense of purpose. God has plans to train and use every one of his beloved children.

Frustration feels like a road-block – but perhaps it's the exact opposite. Perhaps it's God's gift, a pilgrim's humble path that will lead me towards my destiny.

## *For reflection*

**1** Were you surprised to see what the Bible says about work and rest?

**2** Do you think that pacing might benefit you?

**3** Try making a plan for the next big event coming up, even if it's a while away.

*It is wisdom to take occasional furlough. In the long run, we shall do more by sometimes doing less. On, on, on for ever, without recreation may suit spirits emancipated from this 'heavy clay,' but while we are in this tabernacle, we must every now and then cry halt, and serve the Lord by holy inaction and consecrated leisure. Let no tender conscience doubt the lawfulness of going out of harness for a while.*

CHARLES SPURGEON, *Lectures to My Students*, 161

*Do small things with great love*

MOTHER TERESA

*Sometimes we choose our challenges and sometimes our challenges choose us. What matters is our response.*

MARK POLLOCK, severely disabled adventurer

# HAND TO HAND COMBAT

## SYMPTOM MANAGEMENT

Nobody loves a symptom. I've often thought that if this or that symptom would just push off, I'd get on much better with being ill. Sadly, it's part of the deal. There's nothing easy about confronting stubborn symptoms, day in, day out. So I've looked long and hard for effective ways to engage with the enemy.

The principles of pacing from the last chapter also apply to symptom management, so we have a flying start. I'm going to start with pain and fatigue, because either or both crop up in a very wide range of illnesses. Even if you've been spared the Big Two, read on; these ideas apply to handling other symptoms too.

## PAIN

Pain is exhausting, scary and depressing. Nobody sees it and nobody can truly understand how it feels. It's hard to think about anything else. The more I focus on the pain, the bigger it seems to get and the smaller I feel.

It's time to fight back. Imagine building a wall against the pain, using small stones. Each stone is too small to make a difference alone but together they make a solid shelter. Here are some stones to build a wall. As with anything else in this book, please check with your doctor before making any major changes.

> ✳ Shrink the problem. Some pain is there as a warning and some pain is just there. If you're afraid of what the pain might mean, ask questions until you understand what's going on. It takes a lot of pressure off to stop worrying and get on with handling the pain you feel.

* Become an expert. If you have more than one kind of pain, look at each one separately for this step. Listen carefully to your pain, noting what makes it better or worse and any regular patterns. Talk to your doctor and look for good books, leaflets and patient information websites. Find out how and when to use your medication and about possible side effects.

* Rest. Pain zips through your emotional resources and drains your physical energies because of tension in your muscles. Tiredness then makes pain worse. Think about the best position, place, temperature and timing to get the most out of your rests.

* Block the gate. Gate theory says that the nerves which carry pain can't carry more than one impulse at a time. Gently stimulating the area of skin that corresponds with the pain in your body prevents pain impulses from reaching your brain. A TENS machine works this way, by sending harmless electrical signals to the skin through a stick-on pad. TENS machines can be bought, or borrowed from charities or the NHS. Try before you buy, because they don't help everybody. Or go DIY by stroking, tapping or patting your skin. A well placed hot water bottle or wheat bag, ice pack or alternating hot and cold is another way to gate.

* Have fun. It's a relief to enjoy pleasant sensations, which allow your muscles to relax and your fear of pain to recede. Massage or aromatherapy can be a helpful treat. A good TV show, book, music CD or radio programme can take your mind off things. Sexual pleasure, if practical, does it all; it gates, relaxes muscles, distracts and releases powerful pain-killing chemicals in the brain. Having a good laugh or exercising out of doors offers these benefits in different ways. Getting out, socialising or enjoying hobbies, if you can, offers some healthy distraction. Alcohol is a relaxant in the short term but it may not mix with your medication, so please check. Overdoing the booze will definitely make things worse and can cause new pain through nerve damage.

* Care for yourself. Stress, anxiety or depression makes pain feel worse. Having a course of CBT, cognitive behaviour therapy, is one way to regain control over your situation, by updating unhelpful

thought patterns. Or a short course of medication might make all the difference to your outlook. Asking for – or being offered – help with your mindset doesn't mean that the problem's all in your mind. Every part of you is under fire. Remember to care for your spiritual well-being and your relationships too.

## FATIGUE

Illness-related fatigue is nothing like healthy tiredness. It's like a very heavy wet blanket pulled over your head that squashes you flat.

The first thing to do is to listen to your fatigue, however unwelcome its voice may be. Look again at the pain strategy section titled 'Become an expert', above, and assess your fatigue instead. It might help to keep a fatigue diary. If that's too tiring, wait for a good moment and think about the last twenty-four hours.

*"OK, time to get up."*

Pacing works well in managing fatigue. Also, make sure you're managing your illness as best you can in other ways. For example, diabetics with poor blood sugar control are more prone to fatigue.

Try to be reasonable with yourself. Fatigue is a symptom, not a moral failure. My aim is to be a sensible manager of my life as it is now.

### Strength and weakness

I live nose to nose with weakness. I get frustrated every day. I feel the pain as I hit my limits, or make hard choices to stay within them. Of course I long to be strong again. I'd like to have choices and to do things for myself, thank you.

Recently I was wondering if there's any point to this humiliating struggle. Isn't it a waste of my life to be weak? This familiar passage struck me in a brand new light:

> 'Remain in me, as I also remain in you. No branch can bear fruit by itself; it must remain in the vine. Neither can you bear fruit unless you remain in me.
>
> I am the vine; you are the branches. If you remain in me and I in you, you will bear much fruit; apart from me you can do nothing.'

JOHN 15:4–5

Jesus uses the example of a living plant to teach that a man alone is useless, even if he's super strong. If we stop connecting to God and rely on ourselves, we leave behind our chance to bear fruit. Sermons and commentaries tend to apply this idea to proud, rebellious attempts to live our own way. Personal strength becomes weakness in this Bible paradox. But what does it mean for me, now I'm far weaker than I would choose?

It's exciting to grasp the other side of the paradox, where personal weakness becomes strength. The sick have the edge over fit, healthy people because we know we can't manage alone.

So we weaklings are ahead of the game – but there's another step needed for fruitful living. Jesus teaches that we need to be joined to him, like a branch growing on a vine.

The blessing goes both ways. His strength is always available to us and we can offer our weak efforts for his miracle of multiplication. God looks to the heart attitude, so whatever we give willingly he will use for his glory. He has no problem with supplying what we lack, unless we choose to disconnect. It's obvious that any branch that leaves the vine will soon wither and die, bearing no fruit.

Jesus promises that *anyone* who chooses God's ways *will* be fruitful. All we have to do is be joined to Jesus for plenty of fruit to grow at harvest time. This promise is for us and for those who'll enjoy the fruit we bear.

## *For reflection*

**1** Which symptoms are troubling you most? What have you learned about managing them?

**2** Do you think God could use you to bear fruit? What might prevent this harvest from happening, according to John 15:4-5?

*Rivers know this: there is no hurry. We shall get there some day.*

WINNIE THE POOH

*Illness is the most heeded of doctors; to goodness and wisdom we only make promises; pain we obey.*

MARCEL PROUST

*Growth is painful. Change is painful. But nothing is as painful as getting stuck somewhere you don't belong.*

MANDY HALE

*Take the first step in faith. You don't have to see the whole staircase, just take the first step.*

DR MARTIN LUTHER KING JR

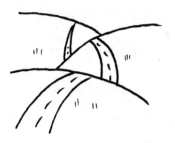

# RHYTHMS OF ILLNESS

*So Potiphar left everything he had in Joseph's care; with Joseph in charge, he did not concern himself with anything except the food he ate. Now Joseph was well-built and handsome, and after a while his master's wife took notice of Joseph and said, 'Come to bed with me!'*

GENESIS 39:6–7

Joseph hit a serious problem after his promotion. Slaves in ancient Egypt were viewed as useful possessions, not real people with their own values and boundaries. They were often married off to other slaves, or taken as concubines, to breed more slaves. So, naturally, Potiphar's faithless wife thought only of her own amusement. She didn't consider her slave's wishes or even his safety. Joseph was forced to cope with celibacy while being sexually harassed.

The story tells us that Joseph bravely resisted the pressure he faced. Potiphar's wife reacted by framing Joseph for rape. Potiphar believed his wife's story and was furious with his faithful slave:

> *Joseph's master took him and put him in prison, the place where the king's prisoners were confined.*
>
> *But while Joseph was there in the prison, the LORD was with him; he showed him kindness and granted him favour in the eyes of the prison warder.*

GENESIS 39:20–21

What a disaster for Joseph, falsely accused and imprisoned without hope of release. But the story shows that he managed not to get stuck in despair or discouragement. The battle for hope was fought in his mind and later revealed by his actions.

Although God had not given Joseph release from his troubles, he still looked after him. Joseph chose to accept this provision in spite of his pain.

Sadly he had plenty of time to think it through. He was locked up for most or all of his twenties.

Peeping forwards into Genesis 41, Joseph's life changed again when he landed a plum job. But under the surface, Joseph knew he could lose it all over again.

## SNAKES AND LADDERS

The sick also live with change, loss of control and difficult questions. How bad will my illness get? How long will it last? Will I regain the ground? Will I die?

Improvement can be stressful too. It's sometimes hard to be grateful when I know it's only temporary. Partial improvement triggers feelings of loss, 'Is this really as good as it gets?' Next comes guilt for being ungrateful. Then I need to rethink my pacing strategies, support levels and planned activities. It's oddly daunting.

Recovery, please God, is a whole new life season. Along with joy, relief and freedom there are drastic changes and new responsibilities. Newly recovered people may find themselves freshly grieving the losses of the past.

This erratic rhythm of good times and bad, remission and relapse, is a challenge to the best of us. So this chapter looks at living successfully with change.

### Taking back the ground

Some days, it helps me to focus on today's unavoidable challenges. If I can make things a little better now, I feel less inclined to fret about the future.

On the other hand, it can help to stand back and look at the whole picture. If your illness involves hospital admissions, perhaps you could use a better period to make a personal admission plan. This could include:

* contact details for people to notify, services to cancel and so on, and the reverse for your discharge
* what you'll need in your bag

✱ if you get ill suddenly, or lack insight when you're ill, a list of danger signs to help others understand your needs
✱ naming a reliable key holder

If you have a plan ready, it makes it easier to get help when you're too ill to explain things. This idea can be modified for a relapse at home, too.

### Busy, busy

The sicker I am, the busier I get. I should be resting – and I do try. But flare-ups mean working hard to cover the basics. When I'm particularly ill, I lie in bed planning what to do the next time I get up. 'Toilet stop, get a drink, phone call, put on the washing . . . oh, it's all too much, I'll just stay in bed.' Indeed, I recently caught myself thinking, 'I need to sleep, but I'm so tired, I need a quick nap first.' I did, too.

Setting priorities gets harder as limits get harsher. It might come down to showering versus eating, or playing with the baby versus paying the gas bill. But these painful dilemmas point to a secret weapon. If we're forced to make difficult choices, we can choose what's most important to us. We do what we decide to do, however small it may be. In a season of loss, this is a way to fight back.

If you're not managing to cover the basics, it's time to act. Asking for help is a sign of maturity. Activate your relapse plan, or start one now. Consider friends and family, neighbours and church contacts. To arrange state-funded home care, start with your GP or social services. A private home care agency is expensive but flexible. How about short-term respite care? Can your patient association, a social worker or a local charity advise you?

Remember to treat yourself well, as you would a sick friend. Personally, I drop most of my standards and give myself little treats during a relapse.

## DAILY BREAD

As time goes by, good strategies for staying upbeat can become stale. A fresh word from God gives new motivation. I find Bible reading makes a difference, even if it feels like a chore at times.

> *I have hidden your word in my heart*
> *that I might not sin against you.*

PSALM 119:11

The word of God offers strength for today and principles to sustain me in future. Reading the Bible is like stocking up my first aid kit. I have no need for a pressure bandage now but if I'm pouring blood, it's too late to go shopping. I need my kit to be ready for life's surprises. Likewise, if my heart is full of good things, I'm equipped to cope when trouble or temptation hits.

A devotional book or system may help you to connect with the Bible. Or try pick-and-mix; reading a devotional, another day reading a Psalm, then moving to read the Gospel you're working through. Memorising verses, if you can, means you have emergency rations on hand if you're too ill to read.

We're all different, so we all have different ways to draw close to God. Perhaps for you it's contemplating nature, quiet reflection, serving others, worshipping with music or something else. If you think about what worked for you in the past, you can adapt it for now. I used to walk alone in green places to pray. Now I talk to God as I tend my plants, sit on my sunny doorstep or watch the clouds sail past my bedroom window.

Suffering and loss also drive me to seek for God. As I endure the silence, I long to hear his voice. When he speaks, it's unforgettable.

One dark night as I lay awake, I reflected painfully that it's hard to juggle the realities of illness with trust in a miracle-working God. I felt so low that I even wondered if it might be easier to face the illness alone. I sensed God gently asking me, 'Emily, do you want me to go away?' My instant response was, 'No!' This midnight meeting built my strength and confidence. It's good to know that my heart belongs to God in the hardest of times.

## WATCH OUT FOR DEPRESSION

Danny enjoyed running his own business. Then he took ill and had emergency heart surgery. Danny fretted at home for months, while his family struggled to keep the business going. Danny felt lost and useless. Over time he became irritable, sleepless and tearful. His alert GP diagnosed depression and started treatment, which worked well. Danny may never be a patient patient, but now he's free to enjoy what's good.

Every ill person is at extra risk of depression, because of the stress of illness. This is called inter-current depression and it's surprisingly common. I found that depression made a bad situation impossible, so it's worth checking. Being ill feels awful, but there's a difference between being distressed and being depressed.

Those of you whose core illness is depression will know all about it. The rest of us can learn to look out for any or all of these things:

* loss of motivation
* loss of hope and vision
* spiritual difficulties
* anger
* irritability
* sleep disturbance
* regular mood changes through the day
* shame
* guilt
* no feelings
* digestive changes
* weight changes
* low libido
* suicidal thoughts
* preoccupation with death
* no pleasure in things you used to enjoy

If in doubt, your GP will help you with this assessment process. Getting treatment for depression doesn't imply that your other illness is 'all in your mind'. Anyway, who needs that old prejudice? Get help, get better and release energy to meet your challenges.

### Not just in your mind

Depression deeply affected my spiritual life for a time. The symptoms of misplaced guilt and shame dried up my confidence in God's love. I found great comfort in a personal survival story, told in Psalm 73 by a man called Asaph. Here's a key passage:

> *When my heart was grieved*
> *and my spirit embittered,*
> *I was senseless and ignorant;*
> *I was a brute beast before you.*
>
> *Yet I am always with you;*
> *you hold me by my right hand.*

PSALM 73:21–23a

The difference between a person and a brute beast (animal) is that people have spirits that can connect to God. As Asaph slipped into depression, he found he could no longer sense God's presence or hear God's voice. For Asaph, as for me, this felt like the last straw.

It helped enormously to know that I was not the only one. I looked into it and learned that this apparently spiritual problem is a common symptom of depression. The heavenly silence would later end as my depression lifted. I agree with Asaph; God was present all the time.[4]

If you're really low and you feel like harming yourself, please get help *today*. Sharing the burden, getting proper treatment and perhaps extra support will point you toward the light. Ring a help line,[5] a friend or your GP and don't give up till you've spoken to someone. You really do matter and there is hope, whatever your feelings tell you.

### New ways to avoid depression

I've known for many years that I'm at risk of low mood during the dark winter months. In the past I took brisk lunch time walks, braving the winter weather to exercise, enjoy nature and get some daylight on my face.

This worked well until I got ME. My life got a lot harder, while exercise and the great outdoors moved out of bounds. Several winters were dogged by painful depression, on top of major physical challenges.

---

[4] Read more about Asaph's inner struggles on p 85, 'Resentment'.
[5] One helpline that's always open is Samaritans, 08457 909090.

I started searching to see what works for me. Nowadays I take St John's Wort all winter long, read under a daylight bulb and inhale clary sage essential oil. Any winter outing tends to be arranged around daylight hours and I spend time indoors beside a window where possible. I've learned to combat my Seasonal Affective Disorder despite having ME. I no longer dread the winter coming and my physical problems feel less overwhelming because my mood is stable.

## FIGHTING OFF BOREDOM

Leona cares full time for her daughter Jan, who fell ill in her teens. Leona comments, 'My main job with Jan is to keep her sane, to entertain her and keep her upbeat until they find a cure.'

I admire Leona's clear-sighted devotion to Jan's mental health, alongside caring for her physical needs. It seems somehow less noble to entertain myself – but why? It's part of managing my illness. Boredom leads to frustration and low mood and eats away at self-respect. If watching a mindless but cheery TV show stops me from slipping into despair, it's a worthwhile activity.

Here are some things I do when I'm not well enough to get moving:

* Remember. Put yourself back into a happy experience. What can you see? Who's there with you? Are there any sounds, textures or smells to enjoy? Slowly take yourself through the memory, savouring every drop.

* Think about your next project, thinking through each step and making choices along the way. You can always change your mind later.

* Make plans. What will you get for someone (or yourself) for Christmas? Mentally redecorate your room, or go from bed to sofa and do the whole house. Plan your next adventure, be it a phone call, a new outfit, a holiday, or tomorrow's TV. Plan a huge adventure, up to and including interplanetary travel.

✳ Imagine a better view from your window, choosing anywhere in the world. Or mentally move house, choosing the room layout and décor. Online estate agents are good for this; no need to budget, for once.

✳ Contemplate what goes into the perfect version of your favourite dish.

✳ Engage your senses; light a scented candle, wrap up in a soft blanket and listen to music.

✳ Count your blessings.

✳ Imagine a conversation with an interesting person, alive or dead. What would you ask? How might they reply?

✳ Consider a dilemma or problem faced by someone you know. Is there a way round it? Is there any small thing you could do? Praying for others is a great help, if possible, as it breaks the isolation.

*"Don't disturb mummy, she's decorating the living room."*

### Day off Lite

In a previous book I suggested the idea of a partial day off for those who have caring responsibilities[6]. This idea also works a treat for those too ill to rest properly.

To start, pick a day of the week. On this day, ignore any tasks that could wait till tomorrow. Take the easy option for everything and use any spare energy for having fun. You might have a pyjama day, eat easy meals or take a day off from your exercises. You could choose a special book or video, or enjoy a phone call or outing.

It works because the change of pace is refreshing. Even if your day off is mostly in your attitude, it's worth doing. It can help you to work hard at your life on the other days of the week and also gives you back a weekly rhythm. Remember to integrate this idea with your pacing strategy, which is covered in Chapter 3.

Your carer also needs a day off, of course, though perhaps not on the same day. There's more about looking after your carer in Chapter 15.

## THINKING STRAIGHT

Without daily work or exercise to bring healthy tiredness, sleep can be hard to find; symptoms can also disrupt sleep. It's very tiring to lie awake hour after hour without respite from discomfort. I find it's easy to end up thinking negatively.

The morning brings the consequences. I start my day drained and irritable, poisoned by my night time thought patterns. To cure my mental hangover I need to go to God, repent and receive cleansing and comfort. I know it would be better if I avoided this toxic cycle but it's very tempting at 2 am. This is a secret battleground, hidden to others while the results are obvious.

> *Above all else, guard your heart,*
> *for everything you do flows from it.*

PROVERBS 4:23

---

[6] Emily Ackerman, *A Time to Care*, IVP.

This verse tells me to carefully protect what goes on and what goes into my heart. It's very easy to fall into a negative attitude, with negative moods, negative choices and a negative life following on. So it's a worthwhile battle to keep my attitudes in good shape. For those of us who can't do much physically, the inner life is even more important. If my mind is a cinema, what's showing tonight? Would I want anyone else to see?

Here's Paul's take on this:

> *Finally, brothers and sisters, whatever is true, whatever is noble, whatever is right, whatever is pure, whatever is lovely, whatever is admirable – if anything is excellent or praiseworthy – think about such things.*

PHILIPPIANS 4:8

Paul is quite clear about our responsibility to choose our focus, whatever the circumstances. The devil is waiting to fill my head with rubbish, if he can find space for it. Experience will show each one what works and what weakens. Like choosing a balanced diet, we need to seek out what we need as well as what we fancy.

Mental illness makes this area even harder. Acute flare-ups may mean giving up the fancy stuff, retreating to a safe corner and waiting out the storm. Still, it's worth looking for some small way to let the fresh air in.

## *For reflection*

**1** Does your illness have ups and downs? What, if anything, triggers these changes?

**2** Make a happy box, a simple personal resource that will bring a smile to your face on difficult days. Find, ask for or buy a suitable box, around shoebox size, and decorate it to look happy. Perhaps a child could decorate your happy box for you. Start collecting anything that makes you smile, such as cartoons, greetings cards with encouraging messages, photos, artwork, invitations, news items, Scriptures or quotes. Your collection can grow over the years.

3 Looking at the section on depression, how would you assess your mood at present? If you're unsure, ask a good friend or check with your GP. This is one burden it's worth trying to budge.

4 What's on your mind? Is it helping or hindering?

*God has not gone away, no, God has not gone away.*

TRADITIONAL KENYAN SONG

*Nobody is bored when he is trying to make something that is beautiful, or to discover something that is true.*

WILLIAM INGE

*Think great thoughts but relish small pleasures.*

H. J. BROWN JNR

*God never places us in any position in which we cannot grow. We may fancy that He does. We may fear that we are so impeded by fretting petty cares that we are gaining nothing; but when we are not sending any branches upward, then we may be sending roots downward. Perhaps in the time of our humiliation, when everything seems like a failure, we are making the best kind of progress.*

ELIZABETH PRENTISS

# A PLACE OF REST

If you're ill, you have to be ill somewhere. You may be in hospital, residential care, living with others or living alone. Wherever you are, there's plenty you can do to enrich your environment so you can rest, heal and enjoy what's good. This chapter looks at customising your surroundings to suit you and your current lifestyle.

## TIME FOR BED

For many of us, the bedroom becomes a place to live rather than somewhere to go at midnight. So it's worth giving the set-up some time, money and thought, like planning a busy home office or kitchen. Here are some simple, affordable ideas for perking up your bedroom.

### The bed

* A sturdy bed with a decent mattress needs to be high up on the priority list.
* A bedside table or box will hold your needs within arm's length.
* Setting yourself up with a phone, notebook, radio or music system (or the remote) within reach offers a change of activity within getting up.
* A pencil writes at any angle, so is better than a pen for writing in bed. A clipboard is good, too.
* I have a soothing CD of ocean waves, set on repeat play all night to counteract any annoying noises that might wake me up. A mobile phone app is another way to provide this – search for baby sleep sounds.
* A comfy chair for you or a visitor is useful. It could be a folding picnic chair stashed under the bed if space is tight.

* A low energy bulb in the bedside light warms up over a minute or two and eases you from dark to light.
* Whatever you do, make sure the bedroom ceiling is painted properly. I did a hasty job of redecorating a bright green ceiling when I was well. Then I fell ill, took to my bed and lay looking at the patchy paint job for fifteen years. Painful.

### The view

* Looking at clutter is draining. Try a box under the bed, or pulling a curtain over the mess.
* Move the bed across the room for a different outlook, or put your head at the other end of the bed.
* Temporarily display something interesting or colourful from elsewhere in the house. Recently I hung my new silky top on a hanger, billowing above a warm radiator. It looked just like it was breathing all by itself. Funny, but not very restful.
* A TV or laptop.
* A lit candle makes the room look quite different and scented products offer a fresh smell.

### Gift ideas

* A bird feeder outside your window. You can get small transparent versions that stick onto the window pane with suckers.[7]
* A vee pillow, lap tray or cordless phone.
* New nightwear, especially if you're wearing it all day.
* An e-reader is lighter than a book and keeps your place for next time.
* A plant or a bunch of flowers bring the outside in.
* A coloured light saver to hang in the window.
* New curtains or bed covers.
* A games console, or a new game for it.
* A pinboard can take a changing display of cards, pictures and cartoons to cheer you up.

---

[7] The RSPB website has a selection.

* A fish-tank is relaxing to watch, if there's space, and someone to take care of it.
* Curtain linings or a sleep mask block unwanted light to protect your rest.

## Get moving

Is your home laid out in the best way for your lifestyle? Simone moved to a small flat with a cramped, dark bedroom and a bigger, brighter living room. She asked for help to switch the rooms over and now spends her days in a double bed in the larger room, complete with a sofa for visitors and bookcases for display. The extra space in bed means she can spread out her projects beside her or have lunch sitting ready on a tray.

If you're able, spending some of the day in another room is refreshing. Camping out on another bed, a sun lounger or the sofa during the day gives a sense of having a defined day and night. Lying in the bath also makes a change of scene, so try to have something nice to look at there too. Would a spell in the garden be an option?

## Personal space

For those in hospital, it's harder to customise your space but even small changes can help.

* Take every opportunity to go to the dayroom for a change of scene.
* Ask to be moved beside a window.
* A postcard or photo could be stuck to the side of your locker.
* Essential oils or perfume can be stashed in your bedside locker to give you a fresh smell to enjoy.
* A small pack of antiseptic hand wipes helps to ward off bugs and smells.
* Earplugs and a sleep mask offer some peace and also signal to staff that you'd rather not be disturbed.
* Could you go home for an overnight or weekend break?
* Is there a church service in the hospital you could attend, or a garden that a visitor could wheel you out to enjoy?

## GOOD IN BED

So now the bedroom is a bit more attractive, what is there available to do or enjoy while ill in bed? Of course this depends on your individual interests and limits – and if anyone shares the bed.[8]

It's good to stay connected with the outside world. Possibilities include phone calls, texts, e-mail from your laptop or writing a short note. Try to make a place for visitors to sit and relax in the bedroom, if possible, so you and they can enjoy a visit more. People may avoid contacting you for fear of disturbing your rest, so tell your friends clearly when is a good time of day to come.

I made a prayer list of people and issues with a paperclip clipped to the top of the list. Whenever I'm able to pray for the person or issue at the top, I slide the clip down to the next one, and I don't forget where I am. It's satisfying and refreshing to intercede for others. It doesn't need to be a long session to make a difference.

### Horizontal hobbies

Hobbies offer a chance to be creative and give a sense of achievement. It may need careful thought to include them into your current lifestyle.

I break my projects down into planning, gathering materials into a box and making stage by stage. Spreading sessions out over several weeks leaves me free to enjoy myself without overdoing. Where's the rush? If it takes longer, it's more fun. But I tend to pick projects with a long deadline. Knitting a jumper for a fast-growing child is asking for trouble.

Thinking things through beforehand has another benefit; time spent enjoying the activity is not wasted by mistakes. This gives scarce energy a big boost.

A really supportive chair (or firm pillows behind your back in bed) and good lighting can take the strain out of sitting up to enjoy your hobby. I often use a lap tray to keep small bits together, perching it on my lap or beside me. Set a timer if you think you'll get sucked in and end up overdoing.

Using paint or glue with toxic fumes needs special planning. Choose a summer day and leave the windows open, or go to another room so you

---

[8] There are suggestions for improving your sex life in Chapter 17.

*"Clive didn't let anything get in the way of his sailing."*

can retreat afterwards. Or take your project out to the doorstep or the garden for the smelly bit.

Consider the possibilities of teamwork. Mary loved making quilts, but with one arm out of action she found certain aspects were beyond her. After much thought, she teamed up with her daughter Dot to produce a magnificent wedding quilt for a friend. Dot cut out the fabric under Mary's supervision and literally lent a hand with other tricky moments. This left Mary to enjoy designing and machine embroidering each square to a high standard, and finally Dot put it all together. Mum and daughter enjoyed their joint project and Mary was able to pass on her skills to another generation.

If you like to make things, you can encourage your friends and make them feel special with a handmade gift. Nobody else has the time these days, which makes a small inexpensive project into a very special gift to receive. I like to pray over gifts as I make them, which adds another opportunity to bless the recipient. If you're making things to sell, you can still pray a blessing over them.

Books can be a great way to escape into another world for a while. Many libraries have a voluntary scheme where you choose your books online or by phone. The books are then delivered (and uplifted afterwards) for you to enjoy at home. Paperbacks are lighter and easier to hold than hardbacks, particularly in bed. An e-reader is even lighter and the font size and screen brightness can be adjusted to suit. If reading is a problem, audio books or large print might help, or try to find the film of the book on DVD.

Watching films on a laptop, or having a TV or computer screen close by, means you don't have to sit up. Paying a monthly rate for instant streamed films or DVDs by post is a possibility. It's cheaper and less frustrating than paying overdue fines because there's nobody available to return the DVDs to the hire shop.

If a film is too long, many TV and radio programs are available online on demand. This is free, no TV licence needed, and there's no pressure to be awake on time for your favourite show. I use this kind of service to watch a program or film in short chunks. I leave it paused and shrunk at the bottom of my screen and hibernate the computer rather than shutting it down. The program will still be there tomorrow.

## BUILD YOUR OWN BLESSING

Recently I had a bad day, the kind where symptoms go up and productivity goes way down. As I lay awake enduring the bad night that often follows a bad day, I felt sad that another day had been wasted. But after careful thought, I realized that good things had happened, hidden between the hard bits. The good things were small, sometimes very small, but small choices and discoveries build into bigger blessings over time.

I was reminded of the ancient Christian discipline of Examen, which reflects on each day in the light of the Holy Spirit. Various denominations have re-interpreted Examen since Ignatius first proposed it four hundred years ago. The idea is to look back carefully at your day, making sure you are listening to what God is saying and doing in your life and noting the choices you made. In this way you become more alert to what's happening and more aware of the presence of God in the everyday details of life.

There are five steps to follow:

1. Become aware of God's presence.
2. Review the day with gratitude.
3. Pay attention to your emotions.
4. Choose one feature of the day and pray from it.
5. Look toward to tomorrow.

Back in bed, as I saw my day from this new angle, I found myself encouraged. I had after all learned something, reinforced some good life choices, experienced moments of joy and chosen to cooperate with God. This led to a loving, thankful conversation with God, which isn't bad going after three hours lying awake in pain.

If this takes your interest, here are some questions to help you assess your day. You may have to look for tiny pointers.

* What did I learn today?
* Which disciplines or good habits did I work on?
* Did I try to cooperate with God today?
* Did I try to serve others?
* Did I ask forgiveness for any wrongdoing?
* Did I find a balance between complaining and denying my illness?
* Were there happy, relaxed or insightful moments today?

## *For reflection*

**1** Is there anything you could do to cheer up your bedroom?

**2** Is there a way you could still enjoy a previous hobby? Maybe there's a new hobby that you could try out. The standard of the end product is less important than enjoying the process.

**3** Try the process of Examen for size. Are there other questions you'd find useful?

*Lying in bed would be an altogether perfect and supreme experience if only one had a coloured pencil long enough to draw on the ceiling.*

G. K. CHESTERTON

*What do I wear in bed? Why, Chanel No. 5, of course.*

MARILYN MONROE

*Think twice, cut once; think once, cut twice.*

PROVERB

*If people were meant to pop out of bed, we'd all sleep in toasters.*

ANON

# LOOKING AT LOSS

7

When I got my first wheelchair, I was thrilled to be out with the family after a long period of house arrest. I smiled at every passer-by, angled my face to soak up every scrap of sunshine and generally enjoyed my inaugural voyage.

It took several weeks to realise what I'd lost. We could no longer go hand in hand because my husband was round the back, pushing me. People I hadn't seen for a while tended to look right through me, or were so shocked that I ended up comforting them. Everybody towered over me as I sat. So conversations meant talking to a zip or craning my neck to a painful angle. Strangers felt free to have a good stare. Because of all this, I became painfully self-conscious in public, not even sure what to do with my hands.

Then there were the physical problems. Every trip needed careful planning. Minor obstacles like a couple of steps or a stretch of gravel suddenly became huge barriers. I couldn't easily turn around or move a little to see something interesting. I went where someone else wheeled me, like a baby in a pram. And in my mind, I became a disabled person.

There's no getting away from these losses; the contrast between 'back then' and 'right now' is always present. And I don't know if there's more loss up ahead. But I've learned that there are still ways to ease the burden.

## FIRST, KNOW YOUR ENEMY

Losses come in three flavours; fixed, ongoing and partial. To put it another way, there are things I live through, things I live with and things that are never quite the same.

Here are two of Joseph's losses, starting from the moment he realised his cushy life was over:

> *So when Joseph came to his brothers, they stripped him of his*
> *robe – the ornate robe he was wearing – and they took him and*
> *threw him into the cistern.*

GENESIS 37:23–24a

Joseph's robe was a symbol of his father Jacob's favour. When his jealous brothers took it from him, he lost his place in the family and his legal birthright. In 31–35 the brothers produced the blood soaked robe as evidence of Joseph's death, leaving poor Jacob heartbroken.

This event was devastating for both father and son, who tackled their loss in different ways. Old Jacob never fully accepted his bereavement and was left despairing and withdrawn. But after Joseph had grieved he was able to move on, leaving that painful episode in his past. This was, or appeared to be, fixed loss.

Later, Joseph expressed a different kind of loss:

> *'But when all goes well with you, remember me and show me*
> *kindness; mention me to Pharaoh and get me out of this prison.*
> *I was forcibly carried off from the land of the Hebrews, and even*
> *here I have done nothing to deserve being put in a dungeon.'*

GENESIS 40:14–15

In prison, Joseph was forced to live with loss of freedom and doubts about his future. His unfulfilled dreams added to his burden. This is ongoing loss, the kind of loss that's in your face, day in, day out. Ever-present uncertainty and pain make ongoing losses truly hard to handle.

## WHICH IS WHICH?

What do fixed, ongoing and partial losses look like for you? Fixed losses might be losing a particular job, opportunity or relationship; having to drop a course or miss a special occasion. Perhaps you've lost a bit of you to surgery, or previous abilities have been permanently damaged.

Ongoing losses include loss of independence or mobility, plus lost opportunities to travel, work, play, date, marry or have children. Then there's loss of life choices or a normal life span.

Partial losses kick in when you still do or have something but have to scale it down because of your illness. Perhaps you're working part-time or in a less challenging job these days, or you can't be so active with the kids. In church, you might sit in a pew instead of taking a lead. With partial losses, letting go of previous glories releases a sick person to make the most of what's on offer now. The only alternative is to withdraw altogether, which seems a bit wasteful.

For example, I grew up steeped in Scottish folk dance. I love the traditional music, familiar steps and the sense of group activity. When I could no longer dance, I couldn't face going to ceilidhs for several years. These days the pain has eased; I sometimes go along, tap my toe and enjoy the happy faces twirling by.

## How long, oh Lord?

Sometimes it can be hard to know whether a loss is permanent. For example, Joseph was reunited with the loving father he had left behind – but he was never free to return to his homeland. As illness changes and new challenges and possibilities emerge, losses can shift and change in your perception.

Strangely, it can be difficult to reconsider a loss when things appear to be improving. Daring to dream again is a costly business. This is why gearing up to a new treatment or going for healing prayer can feel so unsettling.

I find it's a good idea to reassess once in a while, looking at what's lost and what remains. Staying up to date releases fresh energy for the daily challenges of illness. For several years after I'd left my job, I still identified myself as 'a doctor who's off sick right now'. In the end I was able to face the truth, so I said goodbye to my long gone career with many tears. This turned out to be a relief, allowing me to move on to new ideas about meaningful work.

I didn't lose everything from that life season, after all. I still have useful knowledge and my precious memories. I have the benefit of skills gained in those years; for example, my hospital work taught me how to talk to anyone. I met good friends that I still see and I found my husband at university. My past is built in to who I am.

### Repeating patterns

Loss has a habit of repeating, resurfacing like garlic, when I thought I'd swallowed it long ago. It's like a bereavement; the feelings reappear with a tiny reminder of the past. These temporary blips are really painful but they don't mean anything is wrong. Like a tree, I can bend before the wind and then stand straight again without permanent damage.

I know I need to let go of loss over and over, whenever it surfaces. When grieving becomes fixed and stale, I'm really in trouble.

For those with progressive illness, there's a particular problem to face. Fresh loss adds on to old and half-processed losses. That's a complicated mix for anyone to handle.

If you're stuck fast, it might be worth getting some help from a counsellor or minister. Even a very sick person can learn to handle loss more successfully. This restores a bit of control in a horrible life season.

## DENIAL

Denial is a powerful complicating factor when it comes to living with loss. Here's what I've discovered about this unseen enemy.

Denying change is a useful defence mechanism in the very early days of shock and grief. Once it gets to be a habit it turns toxic, blocking good decision-making, growth and joy.

The alternative to denial is facing the pain, which isn't very appealing. But remember that holding back reality is deeply stressful. Medical research has shown that stress can lead to back pain, stomach ulcers, skin conditions and heart disease. Stress weakens your immune system and affects the structure of every cell in your body. It seems that truth will out, in the body if not in the mind.

The root of denial is believing a lie, for example:

*I'm not ill, I'm just lazy. I don't need any help; I can manage by myself. I don't need my medication because I feel fine today.*

### Truth and lies

Lies and false beliefs are a major problem. Satan is the father of lies[9] and he will use this weapon against us whenever he can.

We're all in this battle, although the battleground varies with life circumstances. Here Paul teaches the Corinthian believers how to overcome in this area. He's clearly a veteran:

> *The weapons we fight with are not the weapons of the world. On the contrary, they have divine power to demolish strongholds. We demolish arguments and every pretension that sets itself up against the knowledge of God, and we take captive every thought to make it obedient to Christ.*
>
> 2 CORINTHIANS 10:4–5

It's good to see that we can fight back to defend faith, usefulness and happiness.

While researching this book, I was really struck by the impact of denial on health. I began to prayerfully review my life before and after illness struck. I realised that unresolved difficulties and unchallenged false beliefs may have 'helped' me to fall ill or stay ill. So I'm taking back control of what goes on in my own head. My starting point is reassessing past events. Once I've got up to date, I'll do my best to live in the light of this powerful promise:

> *'Then you will know the truth, and the truth will set you free.'*
>
> JOHN 8:32

Here are some tips on living without toxic denial:

* Try to stay up to date with your life and limits. Things change as you go along.
* Take time to reflect on what's happened. Unexamined loss can drain your energies and trip you up unexpectedly. Would it help to write things down or talk to a trusted friend?

---

[9] John 8:44.

✻ Don't let others take over your mindset. They may wish to avoid facing change or try to force you to face things before you're ready. You're in charge of your process, as they are of theirs.

✻ Grieving takes time and so does handling denial. Give yourself room to breathe; take every opportunity to enjoy what's good.

✻ Bring your burdens to God. He is strong enough to bear them and He can help you find a better perspective.

✻ Try to be specific. Handling one issue at a time makes the process easier.

✻ Wage war on Satan's lies, as Paul explains above. Treat lies like weeds by pulling them out every time they pop up; 'No, that's not true! I don't believe that. *This* is the truth.' Speaking the truth out loud helps to reset your inner soundtrack.

## FINDING FIRM FOOTING

Suffering carries away long-held plans on a tidal wave of uncertainty. People normally assume they're in control of daily life. Illness strips away this comfortable illusion, leaving instead a list of hard questions. Will I get better or worse? Can I cope? What will be left of my life? It seems that any outcome would be easier than the weight of uncertainty.

I've found that even this burden can be put to work. The stress of uncertainty usefully reveals underlying weakness. It's like spotting a crack in the wall that's caused by problems underground. It's never a welcome sight but at least if it's fixed now, it won't get any worse.

Jesus taught that we need eternal foundations to live a confident life:

> *'Therefore everyone who hears these words of mine and puts them into practice is like a wise man who built his house on the rock. The rain came down, the streams rose, and the winds blew and beat against that house; yet it did not fall, because it had its foundation on the rock. But everyone who hears these words of mine and does not put them into practice is like a foolish man who built his house on sand. The rain came down, the streams*

*rose, and the winds blew and beat against that house, and it fell
with a great crash.'*

MATTHEW 7:24–27

My pre-illness foundations rested way too much weight on my role as a
rescuer. When that role gave way I was left unsupported in the storm, like
the foolish man in the parable. You may depend on being or becoming a
good parent, your adventurous lifestyle, or some other foundation. If your
cherished plan comes under threat, it bites deeply into your underlying
feelings about yourself. This season of loss offers a chance to examine what
is holding you up.

Personality type affects the way we handle loss of control. But we're all
in the same boat, uptight or laid-back, well or ill. We all get sucked into
resting our lives on things that won't last. And we all need to upgrade to
solid, eternal rock.

Jesus taught that this means hearing God's word and living it out; in
other words, trust and obedience. This is a major Bible theme, repeated
over and over in different settings. So this painful, messy struggle to follow
God through uncertain times is central to his plans.

## RECYCLED LOSSES

Another life-giving process begins as we learn to offer our lives and losses
to God. As hopeless hurts are laid on the altar of surrender, God can make
something new. Here's Isaiah, foreseeing the powerful ministry of Jesus;

*He has sent me to
… provide for those who grieve in Zion –
to bestow on them a crown of beauty
    instead of ashes,
the oil of joy
    instead of mourning,
and a garment of praise
    instead of a spirit of despair.*

> *They will be called oaks of righteousness,*
> *a planting of the LORD*
> *for the display of his splendour.*

ISAIAH 61:1 and 3

I don't want to miss any of God's provision but if I shut up my heart he will not force his way in. If I can cooperate despite the pain, God promises to replace useless, dusty ashes with beauty. He will transform the sorrowful into majestic, thriving trees. Just imagine what he could do with a bad diagnosis, a sick body, a lost job, a drooping spirit, an overdraft, family pressures or turbulent emotions. This is heavenly recycling, turning rubbish into treasure. Nothing is wasted; every broken thing finds a new purpose.

Challenging denial and surrendering loss are powerful principles from the mighty word of God. They don't take away the pain like a magic pill. Instead, over time they turn the user around into new paths of personal growth. The only limit to this miracle is motivation, which can be truly hard to find. Thankfully, God is patient with his children. He's ready and willing to help us cooperate with him.

## *For reflection*

**1** This idea will help you to handle loss and change, freeing you to live your life as it is now. Make a list of activities and relationships that have changed. Take some time to go down the list and say (or write down) goodbye to these areas. Goodbye to skiing holidays with Pete. Goodbye to my job. Goodbye to always saying 'Yes!' to everything.

**2** Do you think you are affected by denial?

**3** What have you learned lately about your foundations? Are they up to the job?

*Life must be lived forwards, but can only be understood backwards.*

SOREN KIERKEGAARD

*You can clutch the past so tightly to your chest that it leaves your arms too full to embrace the present.*

JAN GLIDEWELL

*Change is inevitable – except from a vending machine.*

ROBERT GALLAGHER

# WORKING ON WORK

*But while Joseph was there in the prison, the LORD was with him; he showed him kindness and granted him favour in the eyes of the prison warder. So the warder put Joseph in charge of all those held in the prison, and he was made responsible for all that was done there. The warden paid no attention to anything under Joseph's care, because the LORD was with Joseph and gave him success in whatever he did.*

GENESIS 39:20b–23

Joseph was a multi-tasking man. Alongside grieving his losses and building maturity and faith, he learned all about prison life. Presently he was running the place. By his daily choices, Joseph had taken control of his painful circumstances. He had a useful job to do and a sense of dignity and purpose.

Joseph's heroic turnaround encourages me to keep trying, even though my career is gone and I have new and difficult daily challenges. Losing my job affected my confidence, motivation, identity and vision. I know I'm not the only one in this fix. So this chapter explores new ways to keep moving, with or without paid work.

## DESIGNED FOR A PURPOSE

In chapter two we looked at why people work and rest. This pattern is built into us:

*So God created mankind in his own image,*
*in the image of God he created them;*
*male and female he created them.*

*God blessed them and said to them, 'Be fruitful and increase
in number; fill the earth and subdue it. Rule over the fish in
the sea and the birds in the sky and over every living creature
that moves on the ground.'*

GENESIS 1:27–28

God blessed humankind with the gift of meaningful work before the Fall;
it's not a consequence of sin. We're perfectly designed to be workers. So it's
no wonder that lack of work bites deep.

In the West, we don't starve if we can't work – but in another way
we're truly deprived. Our culture is obsessed with personal power, wealth
and rank. When these things fall away, we can feel painfully diminished.
This is two edged; it hurts but it also forces us to reassess what really
matters.

God built in the need to rest as well as work. But without work, rest is
hard to find. It seems we enjoy a rest more when we feel it's well earned. So
an ill person with no useful tasks within reach is hit twice over. You and I
still deserve a day off, or a lunch hour, when we stop worrying and striving
and just chill out. Fancy a cuppa, anybody?

## WHO AM I WITHOUT WORK?

I remember leaving my job as a doctor to go on maternity leave. In two
days, I went from directing a team in life-or-death dramas to queuing up
in the Post Office to get my maternity benefit. At that point I realised that
loss of work means loss of role. There was a good reason for the change,
which softened the blow.

A few years later, I found long-term sick leave much harder to face. I
was sinking in a swamp of loss and low self esteem. I urgently needed to
find solid ground, so I started digging deep into the past.

When I was a tiny baby, I was no use to anybody yet precious to God
and to my family, who loved and cared for me with pride. Sadly, children
tend to grow out of the idea that personal value is defined by love. Family,

TV, books, schoolteachers and friends all taught me the same lesson. I must work hard to earn my place in the world.

My illness stripped away my high-status career as a doctor and undermined my role as hard working wife, mother and church member. I had to retreat to daughterhood, to dig deep into the Father's love to retain a sense of meaning.

A few precious people taught me something new. My value *to* them didn't depend on what I could do *for* them. They challenged my self-sufficiency while showing me the scary truth – I am loveable despite my limits.

This crisis triggered a difficult personal journey. I was forced to learn to accept my needy self and to allow others to love the broken Emily. I learned that God's strength is more important than my weakness, although I'm still prone to relapse on that one. I was driven to find rest in God rather than sheltering under my lost abilities. These are uncomfortable, important truths that spur me on to spiritual growth.

### Tricky questions

A little thing like filling in a form reveals my unusual place in society. Which box do I tick? Unemployed, retired, other? Even a simple survey used to make me feel small.

Meeting new people can also be an ordeal as I struggle to answer the everyday question, 'So what do you do?'

These moments highlight my losses but I have a secret weapon. I'm made in the image of God, cherished daughter of a loving Father. That's my heart's true home, not an occupation or role. On the back of that God-given confidence, I've come to rather enjoy the way I don't fit into other people's boxes. Why should I? I'm not square. It's their problem, not mine.

Here's a tip for surviving casual conversations. A question about work is not meant to put you on the spot, however awkward you feel. You could think about other things to say about yourself:

* I like to fix cars
* My interest is in social work
* I'm working towards going to college
* I'm a secretary, but I'm off work at present

* I'm involved with church music
* Right now I'm busy with my brother's wedding next month

You can then move on to ask about what they do or enjoy. They don't need the whole picture right now and you don't have to tell them. They just want a point of contact to continue the conversation.

## BLOCKAGES AND BURNOUT

I learned about another problem faced by the workless sick when I hit an unexpected kitchen sink drama. First the sink waste pipe blocked up, so we had to run the tap into a bowl and pour the dirty water into the toilet. Next, the dishwasher stopped working, so the bowl was extra

*"Have you seen the plunger?"*

busy. The next day the washing machine stopped working. Dirty water backed up into the dishwasher and leaked onto the floor. We mopped up the water with towels but we couldn't wash them properly, so they all went mouldy. The smell of mould spread rapidly and the washing was piling up. Presently the dishwasher got very upset and blew all the fuses, so the lights went out. I hung up the mouldy towels to dry but they just festered on the drying rack. We hastily cancelled all visitors as the smell grew stronger.

We decided it was time for the emergency plumber when the lights went out again. But the socket for the landline was out too; I couldn't even make a phone call. At this point I expected oxygen masks to come down from the ceiling and a recorded voice to say, 'This facility will self destruct in thirty seconds . . . twenty nine . . .'

The plumber confirmed that the only fault was the blocked waste pipe. As the blockage got worse, one by one previously healthy systems and appliances had been nobbled. He unblocked the pipe and left with our heartfelt thanks. We then spent a week drying out the electrics, doing and redoing the washing, cleaning away the mould and airing the flat.

This stressful episode taught me that outflow is vitally important for normal function. Neither plumbing systems nor human beings are designed to take in without passing it on. Ill people can be deeply affected when their talents and energies find no way out. This helped me to understand my struggles with guilt and shame when I was too ill to connect with the world. I became ever more determined to find some small way to serve.

## NO WORK, NO VISION

Another work-related pitfall is loss of life vision. This issue left me floundering in the early years. If I wasn't a doctor and couldn't care for my children, what was the point of being me?

My quest for understanding eventually led me to two hard-hitting proverbs. These powerful verses work together to offer hope and direction;

> *Where there is no vision, the people perish: but he that keepeth the law, happy is he.*
> *A servant will not be corrected by words: for though he understand he will not answer.*

PROVERBS 29:18–19 (KJV)

I could already see that loss of vision means the death of hope and happiness. The verse then explains that living to please God is the path to a better future, even if I can't see the details. The second verse points out that a 'jobsworth' employee will never get close enough to his boss to grasp the whole picture.

Putting these principles together, I realised that any resentful, vision-less sick person who turns his back on God's ways is opting to stay in the pit. Doing the bare minimum is also a big mistake; it's swapping sonship for the servant's place. God is calling his children deeper into his purposes, waiting to teach us the secrets of the family business.

It took me a long time to find, grasp and accept these principles. Eventually I was ready to move my focus from my lost career to the loving priorities of my Father. Taking the first step of obedience opened the door for him to teach me deeper truths about the purpose of my life. I realised that serving God must and could become my life's work.

## TRUST IS THE KEY

Choosing to trust, even a little, allowed me to welcome new ideas. Over time I began to appreciate God's purposes and to rise to his plans. I saw that by clinging to God and learning from him, it's possible to live with vision, dignity and purpose despite the pain of unemployment. This is abundant life, not easy or glamorous but full of meaning.

If your trust has been eroded by painful experiences, like mine, it helps to build bridges in God's direction. It's like repairing a friendship after an argument. What usually works when you're feeling far from God? Attend church, read the Bible, pray, sing, reflect, read books that have helped you in the past, get out into nature, or whatever's possible. Ask friends to pray over this issue for you, too. Although it's hard to push through, the effort builds strength that will come in handy for future challenges.

## WHAT NEXT?

After this, I renewed my search for meaningful, God-directed work that would be manageable within my limits. I found some volunteer work with an email crisis support service, which I could do from home in my better moments. I prayed for others, told them so and asked gently about the results. Eventually I took courage and started writing, just one hour a day, in my dressing gown. These hard-won activities gave me back a sense of usefulness, although I feel frustrated every day by my slow pace.

Other sick people I know have tried freelance work, starting a micro-business, finding a voluntary role in church or community or taking on new jobs within the family. Jim went online and found a good deal for the family summer break, while Grace enjoyed planning her friends' Christmas gifts over several months. Andrew consistently prayed for others – including me, bless his heart – and saved up to give to a good cause.

All this is more important than the visible results might suggest. It allows the sick person to get moving again, to take in and give out as we were made to do. And any step of obedience connects us with the mighty power of God. Our small actions become turbo-charged.

## MONEY, WHAT MONEY?

Then there's the money side of worklessness. Illness can hit loan repayments as well as blowing a hole in day to day expenses. Things will need to change.

If it's time to apply for sickness benefits, or you get turned down, specialist advice makes a big difference. Try looking online for a local Benefits Uptake Officer, Benefits Advisory Service or Citizens Advice Bureau. Your patient association may have specific tips. All this helps you to tell the truth while making the points needed to access a particular benefit. It's worth asking for two copies of the forms, so you can do a trial run and then a good copy to send off. Getting your GP or consultant's support makes a big difference. I went to the surgery specially to ask my GP, politely, if he was prepared to help.

If you're called to a medical assessment or a meeting about your benefits, it pays to bring a witness with you. If you're not happy with what's said, either you or your companion can challenge it. You can ask to see what's being written down and challenge that if necessary. It's not a popularity contest, so do speak up if you feel able.

I struggled with the idea of accepting benefits or services because it challenged my independence. But my taxes had paid for the needs of others over the years, so now it was my turn. I decided that benefits are part of God's provision, gave thanks and relaxed.

It's worth checking any insurance policies or pensions to see how your new situation will affect them. A session with an independent financial advisor offers skilled advice about how to make the most of what you have. A free course on money management helps to ease the transition to a smaller income.[10]

Making changes to suit new spending limits can throw up feelings of loss, shame, fear and sadness. This is hard but it's a normal part of the adjustment process. Many people link their ability to pay their own way with their basic self-esteem. As we've seen, the sick are forced to find their confidence elsewhere.

## WORKING WOUNDED

Of course, some ill people do manage to work. Good for you – but this too has its perils. Returning to a previous workplace brings you nose to nose with new limits. This is painful and frustrating; your colleagues may also find it hard to adjust. Many sick people hide their true state of health at work for fear of being fired, bullied or sidelined. There's more about handling relationships during illness in Chapter 15.

---

[10] Christians Against Poverty offer free money management courses in many areas.

Thinking about your limits can help you find a way forwards. Your patient organisation or union may be able to advise. For example, how about shorter hours, a different chair, a rest area, a new role within the team or flexi-time? Do your homework, speak up and make your case for getting it.

Sunil's back problems severely limited his life for several years. Eventually he recovered enough to return to work. He negotiated reduced hours for his previous job as a senior engineering supervisor, although the effort of working is so great that he can't do much else.

If your previous job is no longer possible, you could look into retraining and moving into another field, or finding a less stressful job with your existing skills. A fresh start might even offer you something your old job did not.

An unexplained gap in your CV is always tricky when you apply for a new job. You could write something about your illness or bring it up at the interview. You can then explain what you can do well, that you've recovered a bit, or however you choose to present your illness. If you don't do this, they might conclude you've been in prison or otherwise up to no good. Talking your way in without mention of illness may be tempting, but if they take you on knowing about your illness, you're on stronger ground legally if you relapse.

Sadly, the effort of working leaves some ill people with no energy for the rest of life. This may be okay for a few months but in the long term it's a killer, especially if you have no help at home. It's hard to contemplate giving up work. But what if you have no strength left over to recover, cook, socialise or clean the house? There are no easy answers, but continuing to work despite all may make your health worse in the long term.

## UNWELCOME TRUTH

As we've seen, illness quickly demolishes personal illusions. Bit by bit, I painfully lost the notion of myself as a stable, brave, good-tempered and loving person. There was the day I suddenly lost my temper with the book I was reading in bed. I decided to throw it across the room to teach it a lesson. I was so weak that it only went a few inches, landing on the duvet to mock my feebleness. Not my finest hour.

I was grateful to find some comfort in Matthew 9. In this story, Jesus goes for dinner at his new mate Matthew's house, along with Matthew's workmates and friends. Jewish tax collectors like Matthew were hated by other Jews because of their corruption, greed and collaboration with the occupying Roman forces. The Pharisees were disgusted that Jesus spent time with these sinful outcasts and openly criticised him. His response strikes a chord with those who have discovered the unpleasant truth about their own weaknesses –

> *'It is not the healthy who need a doctor, but those who are ill.*
> *But go and learn what this means: "I desire mercy, not sacrifice."*
> *For I have not come to call the righteous, but sinners.'*

MATTHEW 9:12–13

Perhaps I need to learn to offer mercy to my newly exposed self. I need expert help from heaven, but that's been true for a while. Doctor Jesus, meanwhile, is quite at home at the bedside of my weakness and failure, ministering healing and covering me with genuine love.

## *For reflection*

**1** If you've had to stop work, think about your previous job. What do you miss? Anything you don't miss?

**2** Now you're ill, what's your version of meaningful work? Is this something you could pray about and explore?

**3** If you're working, how's it going? Is your boss up to speed with what you can do and what you now need at work?

**4** Do you feel able to offer mercy to your new self?

*A diamond is just a piece of charcoal that handled stress exceptionally well.*

ANON

*'Today you are YOU*
*That is TRUER than true*
*There is NO ONE alive*
*Who is YOUER than YOU!'*

DR SEUSS

*Life is so unnerving for a servant who's not serving.*

LUMIERE, 'BEAUTY AND THE BEAST'

*Use what talents you possess; the woods would be very silent if no birds sang except those who sang best.*

HENRY VAN DYKE

*I didn't expect to recover from my second operation but since I did, I consider that I'm living on borrowed time. Every day that dawns is a gift to me and I take it in that way. I accept it gratefully without looking beyond it. I completely forget my physical suffering and all the unpleasantness of my present condition and I think only of the joy of seeing the sun rise once more and of being able to work a little bit, even under difficult conditions.*

HENRI MATISSE

# OUCH! HANDLING EMOTIONS

Being ill is hard work on every level. I find it's easy to end up living on my nerves, placing a huge load on fragile feelings.

This particular burden is difficult for others to see or grasp, which leaves me feeling very alone. For example, I may be physically able to see my old friend Lucy while she's visiting the area. But I know that if I do, her difficult manner will knock my mood and my energy levels right down for days. Lucy's sister, meanwhile, expects me to see Lucy and is cross and mystified when I don't comply. This kind of stress, alongside the 'normal' stresses of ongoing illness, can add up to emotional burnout and further suffering.

It helped me to realise that my reactions to illness were shared by many others. I'm not alone in this battle. So this chapter looks at some common problems; guilt, anger, resentment and self-pity. The next chapter tackles bitterness, lost confidence, frustration and fear.

First of all, there are three questions to ask during any emotional difficulty, to do with faith, lies and symptoms.

## WWJD?

Please don't confuse emotional upheaval with lack of faith or loss of faith. Jesus was the perfect man, yet he wept when his friend Lazarus died, burst out in frustration at the apathy of Jerusalem and roared with anger as he turned the tables of the Temple traders. He got tired, hungry and annoyed with his mates. In the garden of Gethsemane, he felt crushed by the prospect of crucifixion. Our flawless Lord cried out his loneliness on the cross as his Father fell silent. He bore the guilt and shame of all mankind as he died.

This is not a man who spent his time gently smiling, like the Sunday school pictures. Jesus felt and expressed his emotions in a way that was open and authentic, yet lived without sin. I can't expect to do better.

### Is it really me?

Next up, Satan, the father of lies, loves to sneak dodgy ideas into our heads. I find these lies often spark difficult feelings. Lies can be outed by asking two simple questions:

> 'What's the lie?'
> 'Am I disagreeing with God's Word right now?'

So if I feel sad today, what's at the bottom of it? If I'm honest, I feel that God is mean to me and made me ill. Hmm, that sounds a bit like a lie. Now for the truth. Here's what the Bible says:

> Though he brings grief, he will show compassion,
>     so great is his unfailing love.
> For he does not willingly bring affliction
>     or grief to anyone.

LAMENTATIONS 3:32–33

Even if it's a stretch to believe this verse today, it's good to agree with what God says. My feelings and my troubles are not the only things in life. I have God's character and good purposes to rest on.

This simple process usually improves my feelings and I get to build my faith as a bonus. Satan's lies are often blatantly untrue and ridiculous. If you feel bad, it pays to switch on a Scripture searchlight and see if there's a whopper lurking in the shadows.

### Is it my illness?

Illness is obviously stressful and we all react to stress in different ways. But some illnesses directly affect emotions. For example, a diabetic might wake feeling irritable because her blood sugar has slumped, or a depressed man might suffer shame for no reason. These emotions are nothing more than well-disguised symptoms. Patient associations or your doctor can offer advice about this area.

## KNOW YOUR ENEMY

Difficult feelings will drain energy, faith and happiness if they're allowed to take over. Sweeping the mess under the carpet is a bad idea, too. I've learned the hard way that it's best to tackle the problem head-on. The rest of this chapter offers practical strategies for specific emotional reactions. If things are bad, professional advice, medication or counselling may be helpful alongside the medicine of the word of God.

## GUILT

Jo has angina. She often feels guilty. She looks back painfully at missed opportunities and an unhealthy lifestyle. She suffers because she can't manage her messy garden, or mind her beloved grandsons while her daughter goes to work. Then there's the guilt see-saw; pacing versus the 'to-do' list.

Sounds familiar? Here are some ideas to try.

* Diagnose your guilt. Healthy guilt, God-given conviction, is specific. It leads you to act, confessing your sin to God, putting things right and turning away from wrong. Once that's done, it lifts. Toxic guilt, condemnation, is the devil's counterfeit. It hangs over you no matter what you do. It's safe to fight toxic guilt because it's just another lie. Ask a wise friend if you're in doubt.

* Don't brood over your shortcomings. God will show you the truth, if you're open to Him. Here's a useful prayer:

*But who can discern their own errors?*
  *Forgive my hidden faults.*
*Keep your servant also from wilful sins;*
  *may they not rule over me.*
*Then I will be blameless,*
  *innocent of great transgression.*

*May these words of my mouth and this meditation of my heart*
  *be pleasing in your sight,*
*Lord, my Rock and my Redeemer.*

PSALM 19:12–14

* Don't shut God out. Offer him your daily path. He wants to draw close and provide for you in this battle.
* Limit the time you spend thinking about guilt. Crowd it out by focusing on something better.

## ANGER

The root of anger is loss of control. The Bible teaches that it's a human reaction rather than a sin, but an angry person often lashes out with damaging effects. A settled attitude of anger is bad news all round, damaging my walk with God along with my health, happiness and relationships.

### Angry with God

Sometimes it feels like a power struggle is raging. As I face hard times, I'm left trying to balance my 'right' to understand with my need to trust God.

> 'For my thoughts are not your thoughts,
>     neither are your ways my ways,'
>     declares the LORD.
> 'As the heavens are higher than the earth,
>     so are my ways higher than your ways
>     and my thoughts than your thoughts.'

ISAIAH 55:8–9

I'm too limited to understand the ways of God, who expertly manages the universe. It makes sense to submit to him, even when things are confusing and hurtful. I desperately need intimacy with God to survive. Holding grudges against God will poison the relationship, and so will withdrawing in a huff. Another bad idea is denying my feelings because 'I shouldn't be angry with God'.

God doesn't do wrong but sometimes I need to forgive him. In my pain, I've sometimes allowed a warped image of God to attract my anger and hurt. Satan is happy to help, burying my love for God under false beliefs, anger and fear. It's a relief to let go of that wrong perspective. I'm welcome to approach the throne of grace, lay down my grievances and ask him to heal my heart.

> *He is the Rock, his works are perfect,*
> *and all his ways are just.*
> *A faithful God who does no wrong,*
> *upright and just is he.*

DEUTERONOMY 32:4

I've found this verse to be really helpful when anger and mistrust well up. This is the truth, like a cooling ointment.

### Angry with others

If you're angry with a person or system, start by facing your feelings and venting them responsibly, perhaps by writing a letter that you don't send. Next, try to work out how they have taken control away from you and what you can do about it. Armed with this knowledge, it may help to have a careful discussion or send a well-considered letter.

Sometimes anger can be channelled usefully into campaigning for better treatment for the sick, or speaking up for somebody else. This doesn't let us off from trusting God and forgiving the offenders, because these processes are for our good.

## RESENTMENT

Resentment can become an obsession that eats into a sick person's strength, joy and pleasure. It starts with lack of forgiveness. I may fume about specific people who treat me badly, or burn with bad feelings about 'the system'. This mess has to be resolved to protect faith, good relationships and peace of mind.

[11] See also p 43-44, 'Not just in your mind'.

Remember Asaph the Psalmist, who endured a nasty bout of depression?[11] He's an interesting character. He worked as a worship leader under King David and later King Solomon. Asaph was the top man, taking part in state occasions like the dedication of the Temple. The Psalms of Asaph reveal his honesty, his prophetic anointing and a strong sense of justice.

When I looked more closely into Psalm 73, I realised that the reason Asaph got depressed was his epic struggle with resentment. Asaph's senior position meant that he mingled with the rich and famous at the king's court. He noticed that not all of these celebrities were as good as they looked. His troubles really began to bite when he took his eyes off God:

> *Surely God is good to Israel,*
> *to those who are pure in heart.*
> *But as for me, my feet had almost slipped;*
> *I had nearly lost my foothold.*
> *For I envied the arrogant*
> *when I saw the prosperity of the wicked.*
>
> *They have no struggles;*
> *their bodies are healthy and strong.*
> *They are free from common human burdens;*
> *they are not plagued by human ills*
> *. . .*
>
> *Surely in vain have I kept my heart pure*
> *and have I washed my hands in innocence.*
> *All day long I have been afflicted,*
> *and every morning brings new punishments.*

PSALM 73:1–5 and 13–14

Asaph felt that his own faithful lifestyle was apparently unrewarded while his nasty colleagues flourished. Understandably, he hit burnout:

> *When my heart was grieved*
> *and my spirit embittered,*
> *I was senseless and ignorant;*
> *I was a brute beast before you.*

VV 21–22

So poor Asaph slipped from resentment into depression, grief and bitterness.

> *Yet I am always with you;*
> *you hold me by my right hand.*
> *You guide me with your counsel,*
> *and afterwards you will take me into glory.*
> *Whom have I in heaven but you?*
> *And earth has nothing I desire besides you.*
> *My flesh and my heart may fail,*
> *but God is the strength of my heart*
> *and my portion for ever.*
> *Those who are far from you will perish;*
> *you destroy all who are unfaithful to you.*
> *But as for me, it is good to be near God.*
> *I have made the Sovereign Lord my refuge;*
> *I will tell of all your deeds.*

vv 23–28

Asaph started to feel better when he looked for God's loving purposes. He joyfully realised that whatever becomes of his life and his health, God is always with him.

### What can I do?

Here's a pathway for resolving resentment, using the principles of Psalm 73:

* Give yourself permission to honestly think, feel and reflect.
* The more you're hurting, the bigger the need to forgive. You may need to choose forgiveness over and over until you know you're free.
* Resentment is about loss of power. So when you allow your loss to take centre stage, you're giving the offender even more power. This moves your focus away from God, which blocks you from receiving strength from God to tackle the problem. Changing your focus is vital; don't wait to feel better to take this step.

✱ Enjoy the truth. Believers are safely in God's hands at all times. God is King and overrides injustice with his own heavenly agenda. Joseph's story is a powerful example of this.

✱ Make every effort to stay close to God, reflecting on his character and his good plans for you. It's harder work than fuming and muttering, but it pays off richly in new strength and peace.

## SELF-PITY

It's very tempting to feel sorry for myself sometimes. Self-pity looks a bit like grieving over genuine losses, so it can sneak in that way. Once it's in the door, it oozes everywhere and starts to smell bad.

Self-pity cries out to be heard but it's not a genuine emotional response. It's just a trick, Satan's counterfeit of grief. I imagine my self-pity as a big vat of tepid, gloopy school-dinner soup that I have to wade through – or even worse, drink my way out of. After too much time stuck in the soup, this is one temptation I fight without mercy. I've learned the hard way that self-pity saps badly-needed strength and takes the flavour and zest out of life.

I'm far from heroic, in case you hadn't noticed. But if I catch myself in 'Poor Old Me' mode, I try to take action immediately. First, I check that I'm not in need of food, medication or rest. Next, do I have unresolved sadness or pain that needs my attention?

Once I've cared for my needs as best I can, if I still feel blue, I change my focus. I pick up a book or do something useful. I also look around hopefully for a big hug, which I find very effective for soup-stain removal. If I'm too tired to get up and go and nobody huggable is within reach, counting my blessings is hard but gets results. A bit of thankfulness will power wash the soup away, leaving room for healthier things.

### Nobody understands me

Is your illness visible? Mine isn't, unless I'm using my wheelchair, in which case there's no hiding it. Many people with invisible conditions like lupus, depression, ME or brittle diabetes find that this burden is a heavy one.

I thought my friend Mike understood my situation. He was always kind and supportive. Then one day he got annoyed and said, 'But why do *you* get disability benefits?' and my heart sank like a stone. Where do you start?

This isolation is painful and for some reason, leads me particularly close to the self-pity soup swamp. Perhaps it's because the problem itself is so hard to explain. I can only run to God for help.

## MY CROSS TO BEAR

Sometimes I feel I have my hands full just managing my illness. Bearing this load is my service to God. Surely he can't expect anything else from me. Then on particularly grumpy days, I think, 'Well, this is a stupid waste of time, but if I have to do it, I'll do it my way.'

One day I was shocked to realise that this path was running directly away from salvation. I was taking my life back from God into my own hands. Time to think again, despite the pain and pressure.

In Luke 9:18–27, Jesus' disciples had just grasped that Jesus was truly the Messiah. At this high point, Jesus explains his destiny of suffering and death on a cross. He goes on to spell out what's expected of his followers:

> Then he said to them all: 'Whoever wants to be my disciple must deny themselves and take up their cross daily and follow me.'

LUKE 9:23

There are four points that strike me. First, Jesus is speaking to *anyone* who wants to follow him. The sick are not left out.

Next, Jesus said we have to deny ourselves to obey God, regardless of personal wishes, ideas or priorities. This is always going to be uncomfortable, so there's no use waiting for it to get any easier.

The third command is to carry my cross. I guess that's to do with lugging around my illness. But fourthly, and at the same time, I must follow Jesus. This calls for daily, active personal choices. There's no room for dodgy attitudes or hiding from God. Ouch.

The good news is that if I do all this hard stuff, I'll be following God, who lovingly provides for and transforms me. I don't want to withdraw from him into loneliness and spiritual poverty.

When I'm very unwell, it's easy to feel alone in an illness bubble. Hospital stays in particular cocoon patients away from real life. Of course some days will be taken up with the struggle for survival. But the focus of our lives needs to be on our Father's business. We're called to look further than the end of the bed.

## *For reflection*

**1** Think about the last time you got really cross, or felt unexpectedly emotional. What set you off? How did you recover?

**2** What do you think a healthy emotional life would look like for you? Is there one area you'd particularly like to improve?

*Self-pity in its early stages is as snug as a feather mattress. Only when it hardens does it become uncomfortable.*

MAYA ANGELOU

*For every minute you remain angry, you give up sixty seconds of peace of mind.*

RALPH WALDO EMERSON

*It is hardly possible to build anything if frustration, bitterness and a mood of helplessness prevail.*

LECH WALESA, ground-breaking polish politician

*Suffering is humiliating and opaque*

ANON

# MORE EMOTIONS

# 10

Well, so far so good. Next I present my home-baked tips on bitterness, loss of confidence, frustration and fear. I don't live on a fluffy cloud and neither do you. Illness is tough and we suffer accordingly. But there are ways to ease the struggle without storing up trouble for the future.

## BITTERNESS

We've all met bitter people who are locked in their past, holding fast to grudges, self-pity and grievances. Rigid, angry and negative, they often drift into loneliness. Their grievances are treasured possessions but they have little else in life.

It's no wonder Paul spells it out – bitterness is bad news:

> *Get rid of all bitterness, rage and anger, brawling and slander, along with every form of malice. Be kind and compassionate to one another, forgiving each other, just as in Christ God forgave you.*
>
> EPHESIANS 4:31–32

The alternative is love and forgiveness, which is costly because it means letting go of my version of the past. Offering kindness and trying to understand the viewpoint of my enemy is a true challenge. God has led the way, offering grace in the face of repeated offences.

Because bitterness is so damaging, it's worth keeping it out from the start:

> *Make every effort to live in peace with everyone and to be holy; without holiness no one will see the Lord. See to it that no one*

*falls short of the grace of God and that no bitter root grows up
to cause trouble and defile many.*

HEBREWS 12:14–15

So there's the key to seeing God at work in my life: I'm enabled to offer peace to others by staying close to God. These Christlike attitudes can be built like muscles by laying down offence and hurt, time after time. A life free of bitterness is worth some time in the gym.

I had a battle with resentment and bitterness when a doctor refused to refer me for the specialist physiotherapy I badly needed. I felt too hurt to fight and too cross to give in. I spent several weeks throwing tantrums and wallowing in evil thoughts but it didn't bring me any relief. Realising I was turning into someone I didn't like, I decided to push myself in another direction. I grudgingly repented, forced myself to forgive my enemy and weeded out my bitter thoughts before they took root. As a bonus, when I re-channelled all that wasted energy into arguing my case, I won the therapy I needed.

## LOSS OF CONFIDENCE

We've already seen how illness shakes familiar foundations. There are other changes too, like weight gain or loss, mobility and sensory problems, lowered budget and lack of stamina. It can be hard to stay confident with all that going on.

My speech goes haywire when I'm tired, along with my balance, short-term memory and concentration, so I appear to be drunk. I sometimes feel reluctant to leave home, or I avoid busy places or social occasions, in case this embarrassing problem hits.

Low confidence makes it harder to ask for what I need or want. This in turn can sabotage relationships that are already feeling the strain of major change.

Sammy has MS and can't get out much. Here's how he tackles this issue:

*I've lost confidence in all sorts of activities, just because I
so rarely do them. Simple things like going into a shop, putting*

*my PIN into a cash machine or going to social events, all become unfamiliar and scary. I often come back to Isaiah 41:13, "For I am the Lord your God who takes hold of your right hand and says to you, Do not fear; I will help you." I picture Jesus holding my right hand and giving me confidence.*

Where can our confidence safely lie, now things are tough? A passage in Jeremiah offers this beautiful illustration of the truly secure man or woman:

> *But blessed is the one who trusts in the LORD,*
> *    whose confidence is in him.*
> *They will be like a tree planted by the water*
> *    that sends out its roots by the stream.*
> *It does not fear when heat comes;*
> *    its leaves are always green.*
> *It has no worries in a year of drought*
> *    and never fails to bear fruit.*

JEREMIAH 17:7–8

Some days I certainly feel the heat and my leaves start to droop. Jeremiah explains that I need to look to my roots, taking time to build a living, sustaining connection with God.

### Fear of others

Some illnesses trigger paranoia, an irrational fear of hostility or harm from other people. Many other ill people have a milder form of this, worrying over how others will view us or treat us. Of course, sometimes we do face bad treatment.

Late one night, my wheelchair was stolen from our locked communal hallway. The children concerned had recently stolen another wheelchair. They were seen on CCTV the next day, racing the spray-painted chairs along a third floor balcony. At the end of their games, the chairs were dropped onto the concrete path below. My poor battered chair limped home on two wheels, with big red splodges all over it. Even the world-weary police were shocked.

*"I always have the sense that something bad is just about to happen."*

So I was stuck in until a replacement arrived. I found myself lying in bed listening for noises at night. I kept anxious watch when I finally got out and about again. I feared the mini-criminals would tip me out and take the new wheelchair from me in the street. For a while it felt safer to stay in, until I chose to fight back against this new layer of limits over my life.

The core of this fear is expressed neatly in a proverb, along with a secure, eternal remedy:

> *Fear of man will prove to be a snare,*
>     *but whoever trusts in the LORD is kept safe.*

PROVERBS 29:25

Everybody has to face up to fear of man. It's a universal issue that I must handle in my particular setting. To rebuild confidence and unlearn fear of man, I had to change my focus. When thoughts pop up about what others may think or do, I imagine pressing a button to shrink the thoughts down again. The verse above is very useful to bring my mind back in line. I can choose to build my confidence on my Father's great love, instead of the reactions of those around me.

When I face a daunting challenge, I arm myself in all departments. Here are my top tips:

* Remember that you're never alone. God has promised never to leave nor forsake you. (Deuteronomy 31:8)
* Present a confident or cheery first impression. I often wear my favourite purple waistcoat when I feel nervous about going somewhere.
* Break the isolation. Ring a friend and ask them to pray with you. Could someone come with you? Could you plan to ring someone later to tell them how it went?
* Remember that most people are thinking about their own concerns, not other people's.
* If it's something you can put off, choose a small reward to enjoy afterwards, or ask a friend to hold you accountable.

Once it's done, reflect: how did you feel? Was it as hard as you had imagined? What did you learn?

## FRUSTRATION

Illness is deeply frustrating. The weight of this frustration is draining and depressing, day after day. Frustration can lead to fretting and despair, or it can spill out as anger, cynicism or irritability.

Frustration sets in when we don't get what we want. This sounds a bit childish, but the frustrations of the sick are nothing like a toddler tantrum, or a busy man who swears at a red traffic light. Our frustration is triggered by limits rather than immaturity. It's related to the ongoing losses of illness, which can't be resolved and left behind. This link with loss reveals why our frustration is so hard to shake off.

Jim is very immobile due to advanced motor neurone disease. He comments, 'If I need my itchy nose scratched and my carer asks me to wait a minute, that *wait* feels like a *weight* on my shoulders. I'm so tired of carrying these heavy waits.'

Fluctuating illnesses are famous for triggering frustration. The things I could do yesterday are impossible today, regardless of my plans. Then on a better day, other factors may make my plans fail. Even living with the burden of frustration can feel frustrating. This has been my biggest struggle in the area of emotions.

To be honest, at times I've felt as if God doesn't care. Nothing about my life is hidden from him but he doesn't seem to intervene. During a particularly poorly phase, I became hurt and indignant at God's stillness. Did I really want to follow this God, who sees all and yet does nothing? I felt like an orphan, abandoned and unwanted; or even worse, that God was watching my every move with a hostile and judgmental eye. When I realised that this same God was the only one who could heal this hurt, I felt exposed, humiliated and powerless. This was the darkest pit of all.

Looking back, this was a God-ordained opportunity to die to myself and take the way of the cross. Jesus was so weakened by his suffering that he was forced to ask Simon to carry his cross for him. I see now that I was right there on that bloodstained road, following Jesus.[12] I wish I'd grasped this at the time. I felt like a failure and a disgrace; weak, ashamed and far from God. I had to dig deep and decide what I really wanted, before gathering courage to ask him for help with my attitude. Over time the burden of pain started to lift, although the frustrations remain.

### Fighting frustration

Paul teaches that frustration is a natural part of life in a fallen world, where we all live with painful restrictions:

> *I consider that our present sufferings are not worth comparing*
> *with the glory that will be revealed in us. For the creation waits*
> *in eager expectation for the children of God to be revealed. For*
> *the creation was subjected to frustration, not by its own choice,*

---

[12] Mark 8:34 and Matthew 27:32.

*but by the will of the one who subjected it, in hope that the creation itself will be liberated from its bondage to decay and brought into the freedom and glory of the children of God.*

ROMANS 8:18–21

Frustration for the well is often seen as a temporary nuisance, or an opportunity to build character on the road to greatness. For the sick, the struggle with frustration and loss is more like a never-ending battle.

Here are some tips from the battlefield:

* ✳ God looks at the heart attitude, not the outward appearance. Give yourself a pat on the back for holding a good attitude, or refusing to complain.
* ✳ Take a break. Find another focus. Get moving, if possible. Read a book, go out, move to another room, brush your teeth or sing.
* ✳ Laugh as much as you can.
* ✳ Name your issue to shrink it down. 'I can't do *anything!*' becomes 'Today I can't post Tom's birthday card and nobody's here to help me.'
* ✳ Get creative. Can you find a way around this problem, now or in future?
* ✳ Have a nap. Frustration is exhausting. It might look better in the morning.
* ✳ Embrace the inevitable. God has allowed today's difficulty. He is ready to help you grow towards maturity.
* ✳ Be your own friend. Forgive yourself when you can't manage something you wanted to do.
* ✳ Don't pile on shame or guilt. You're facing difficult times and it's natural to feel frustrated. God loves and understands you.

## FEAR

Illness poses frightening questions and dilemmas. Am I going to die? Will I ever recover? Will my loved ones stick around to look after me? How will I pay my rent now I'm not working?

Unchecked fear adds a crippling new layer of limits, so it has to be worth some attention. But there are other areas also needing work. Good illness management calls for facing the truth and taking care of myself. So hiding my fears behind denial or self-neglect is pointless, like moving my rubbish to a different room.

### Why am I afraid?

I'm regularly ambushed by anxieties and fears. I have poor balance, so even if I'm not falling, I'm taking anxious care to avoid a fall. Another fear flashpoint is dealing with social occasions. Then there's the state of our bank balance. These are everyday stresses that can only be avoided by hiding under the duvet – and I spend enough time under there as it is.

So I've thought a lot about conquering these fears. Fear is a natural response. It focuses my mind on a threat, so I can take action to keep safe. But what happens if I can't take action? If my illness prevents me from acting? I'm left with fearful feelings.

The root of fear is not in the threat itself but in my reaction. After all, if I didn't know about this threat, I wouldn't feel scared of it. This means that if I can tackle my reactions, I can fight my fears.

At a deeper level, fear feeds on a self-centred mindset. The focus is on my small resources and my big concerns. It's all about me. This perspective drives a wedge between me and God, which then blocks God's provision for my crisis. This is why the devil is so keen to tempt me into a pit of fear that shuts out the light.

### A lifeline for the fearful

1 Peter 5:1–11 signposts five steps from fear to faith. Peter offers practical strategies for people facing tough times:

> *All of you, clothe yourselves with humility towards one another, because,*

> 'God opposes the proud
> but shows favour to the humble.'

*Humble yourselves, therefore, under God's mighty hand, that*
*he may lift you up in due time.*

vv 5b–6

Step One is to address my self-centred mindset and move the focus outwards. Others may have a point, after all. God is bigger than anything I face and his ways are better than my ways.

*Cast all your anxiety on him because he cares for you.*

v 7

Step Two, let God take the strain. If I lapse and pick up those burdens, I can lay them down again. Like forming a habit, it takes time to break the old pattern and stick with the new.

That's good, but I'm not finished yet.

*Be alert and of sober mind. Your enemy the devil prowls around*
*like a roaring lion looking for someone to devour. Resist him,*
*standing firm in the faith . . .*

vv 8–9a

Step Three is actively resisting the devil's attempts to control me with fear and worry. Peter continues,

*. . . because you know that your brothers throughout the world*
*are undergoing the same kind of sufferings.*

v 9b

It feels like a lonely struggle but there are others out there, working hard to stay afloat. Peter explains that better times will come:

*And the God of all grace, who called you to his eternal glory in*
*Christ, after you have suffered a little while, will himself restore*
*you and make you strong, firm and steadfast.*

v 10

Step Four is restoration. I'll get stronger as I cooperate with God, so the battle is truly worthwhile.

*To him be the power for ever and ever. Amen.*

V 11

As the passage closes, Step Five is not about us, our struggles or the devil's schemes. The spotlight is on God in all his power and glory. May it be so in our lives.

## *For reflection*

**1** Take some time to tell God about how you feel today.

**2** Is there anyone you need to forgive today? Choosing to forgive them doesn't imply that they are blame-free, or that what happened was acceptable. It's a way of resolving the past that also releases God's forgiveness and healing over both of you.

**3** Write down the things that drag you down. Lay the list in front of you and visualise unloading these burdens one by one into God's strong arms. Tear up the list and give thanks.

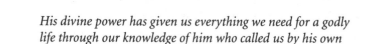

*His divine power has given us everything we need for a godly life through our knowledge of him who called us by his own glory and goodness.*

2 PETER 1:3

*She prayed that the breath of God would blow cleanly through her heart, that she would have the strength to stand in the face of both its turbulence and stillness, that her heart would remain an open place, and that the wind that blew bitter sorrow and grief into her heart would also take them away.*

MARELE DAY, MRS COOK

*Bitterness? I don't have time to be bitter. There's far too much to be done.*

NELSON MANDELA

*God moves in a mysterious way His wonders to perform;*
*He plants His footsteps in the sea and rides upon the storm.*
*Deep in unfathomable mines of never-failing skill*
*He treasures up His bright designs, and works His sov'reign will.*

*Ye fearful saints, fresh courage take; the clouds ye so much dread*
*Are big with mercy and shall break in blessings on your head.*
*Judge not the Lord by feeble sense, but trust Him for His grace;*
*Behind a frowning providence He hides a smiling face.*

*His purposes will ripen fast, unfolding every hour;*
*The bud may have a bitter taste, but sweet will be the flow'r.*
*Blind unbelief is sure to err and scan his work in vain;*
*God is His own interpreter, and He will make it plain.*

WILLIAM COWPER

Cowper's mother died when he was six. He was bullied at boarding school, most of his siblings died in childhood and his family stopped him from marrying the woman he loved. Cowper had a lifelong battle with severe depression and doubts about his salvation. He wrote this beautiful hymn in 1773 as he entered one of his depressive states.

# WHAT ABOUT HEALING?

The Bible is full of healing miracles – so I want one too. This is a controversial and mysterious area, with plenty of strongly held opinions on offer. When someone is healed it's truly wonderful, but what about the others?

I believe we're all in it together, well or ill. We're living in a troubled, fallen world. We've seen our minor injuries and hurts naturally healing up. So we can all give thanks for past healing. And everyone can benefit from bringing unhealed wounds to God.

This chapter is aimed at building understanding, hope and encouragement, come what may. For starters, here are three painful questions often faced by the sick.

## WHY ME? WHY HIM?

Prayer for healing may bring improvement, complete recovery, or no visible results. The apparently random nature of the process can raise painful issues. When I'd been ill for two years, my husband also developed a similar illness. After three months of crisis at home, our church lovingly fasted and prayed over us as a family. The effects were immediate. My husband rapidly recovered, while my ME got worse. I was left behind, alone in the double bed like someone on the wrong end of the Rapture. I was crushed, my husband developed survivor guilt and the church was left wondering what had just happened.

I had so many unanswered questions. Had I failed in some way? Was this really God's plan? Feeling alone, hurt and afraid, I fell for Satan's lies:

'My husband is more important to God than I am, so he got healed and I didn't.'

'God has to love me but he doesn't like me very much. He punished me by showing the world how little he thinks of me.'

I was in a bad way so let that stuff take root. The Bible teaches a very different story, one of God's love and mercy. I should have known better but I couldn't face the uncertainty. I settled for the wrong answer to avoid trusting God with no answers in sight. Satan was happy to supply the lies, of course, so he could sit back and watch them nibble away at my foundations.

I'm still working on this experience, which knocked my confidence for a very long time. These days, I'd rather leave room for God's mysteries than buy in to Satan's lies. Everybody has loose ends to handle, so it's not just me.

## IS IT MY FAULT?

Christians sometimes fear that their unhealed illness is a punishment, or the consequence of sin. In the early months of my illness, this fear triggered long hours of painful introspection and repentance. After a while I realised I had done everything I could about my past failings. It was time to move on. My burden lifted when I read Hebrews 12, which explains that God disciplines his children for their own good:

> *Endure hardship as discipline; God is treating you as his children.*
>
> HEBREWS 12:7

Discipline is a much more positive business, to do with preparing for the future. It's all about love, training, guidance, mentoring and plenty of opportunities to build strength in a particular area. We have nothing to fear from our Father's wise discipline, even when it hurts for a time.

As for illness as the consequence of sin, watch out for condemnation. After all, everybody is sinful but not everybody is sick. Even where sin is clearly the cause, God has made a way for us. Any sinner can repent, be forgiven and live confidently in the sunshine of God's favour.

## 'WHAT HAVE YOU GOT TO LOSE?'

For those who hope to be healed, there's an issue that's hard for the well majority to understand. Reaching out for change brings uncertainty and undermines precious peace of mind. Dreams are like tents – easy to get out of the bag but very hard to fold up small and pack away again. So it can be difficult to face an opportunity to receive healing prayer, yet unpopular to refuse it. This painful predicament is not the same as lack of faith.

It's hard to know when to stop praying for a specific healing in the face of no apparent results. Balancing perseverance with submission is a tricky thing to do, particularly when you feel hurt and disappointed.

*"OK, let's put it back into the bag."*

For both these issues, there is no shortage of people who think they know what's best for you. Jumping through hoops to please others may not gain you anything but exhaustion.

There are no easy answers here. Only you know what you can handle and what you feel is right before God. He's still with you, caring for you through the pain.

## FIRM FOOTING

So with all this uncertainty to handle, where's the solid ground? There are two principles that will support any sick believer; personal healing capacity and God's master plan.

### Everyday miracles

Sammy broke his leg when he was two and was plastered from toe to hip. He was unable to stand or walk, and sat pointing at his leg, saying sadly, 'Broken!' His parents assured him that it would get better, but in his experience, broken toys stayed broken and got thrown away. No wonder he was upset.

Sammy made a full recovery through God's healing power, built into his body before birth. We're all equipped with an amazing ability to repair our bodies and minds. If not, every single cut, bruise, infection, scare or sadness you've suffered since birth would still be hurting you.

Even when things go badly wrong, the human body makes a valiant attempt to fix itself, given time, rest and nourishment. I've never understood why this personal healing capacity is seen as separate from God's healing miracles. It looks like a miracle to me.

### God's perfect plan

What happens when I pray for healing? God hears and answers, but often I'm not asking with an open mind. God responds with 'Yes', 'No', or 'Later', according to his plan. An unwanted answer often triggers disappointment, but this process isn't finished yet. He's looking at the long term, beyond today's urgent request.

Prayer is a conversation, so God listens for my response as I listen for his. If I try to block out God's voice, or go into a huff at his response, I risk making an adventure with God into a lonely trial. On the other hand, responding with submission and trust gives God freedom to reign powerfully over my circumstances. He always has something good in mind for me.

### I still belong

The principles of personal healing capacity and God's masterplan helped to rebuild my lost confidence and joy. Unhealed Christians are not rejects or misfits; God is safely in control. What a relief!

My next step was to widen my scope, taking a different attitude to God's purpose and power. I had asked God to help and heal me but his agenda came as a surprise. God knew that illness is not the only problem.

### Who's in charge?

Here's a prayer I've prayed many times with no success: 'Lord, please heal my body today. I want to return to my previous way of life.'

It looks okay, but here's the problem. I made my request really specific, with terms and conditions at the end. It may be impossible or unsafe for God to say 'Yes' to this prayer, even if he wants to bless me with physical healing at this time.

What if my previous way of life was physically, emotionally or spiritually unhealthy? If God did just what I asked, I would soon get sick again, or come down with something even worse. I may need to address other issues first, to allow my healing to arrive and stay for good.

It's easy to say that I would cooperate with God over my issues once I'm well again, but he knows my heart. Perhaps I need the motivation of my illness to push me through the hard stuff. Or maybe God needs to do things in a certain order. Maybe healing my illness is not on his agenda for me right now. When I pray so narrowly, it's easy to misinterpret a 'No' answer from God, leaving me hurting and sad.

Sometimes it's right to pray specifically. But for me, praying in this way was an attempt to take control. I suspect I was blocking God's blessing by my attitude, even as I cried out for his help.

## FACING THE GOBSTOPPER

Living with challenge is normal, even though I feel stretched at times. Living with unhealed hurts, bad attitudes and hidden sin is another matter, holding me back from abundant life. This reminds me of gobstoppers, those big round sweets I ate as a child. There were lots of hard multicoloured layers to be sucked off one by one, and in the middle was a little piece of chewing gum. The challenge of illness is the chewing gum, the bit in the middle. That's enough for anyone to chew, without layering on hurt after hurt until it gets big enough to choke on.

These gobstopper layers of hurt and sin have distinct flavours, some of them self-indulgently sweet and others bitter or sour. If I ignore them, they'll stick around and more layers will build up on top. Sometimes I've needed others to help me with this process.

*"Would you like some help with that thing?"*

It's not easy to face my weaknesses, or to ask for help. But whether or not God is planning to release me from illness now, he has good plans to bless, encourage and free me now. So I don't want to miss out. There's no need to go digging. God will show me what I need to know, if I let him in.

## Let God be God

*Submit yourselves, then, to God. Resist the devil, and he will flee from you. Come near to God and he will come near to you.*

JAMES 4:7–8

According to James, God's way looks like this. We come to God as we are – in my case, weary, ill and fed up. We give God room to move, free from our agendas. God might choose to begin with fears, impatience, eating habits, hurts, grudges or other human weaknesses that need his expert attention.

Maybe you feel there's no time for this; you need healing now to survive your illness. If that's you, meet Esther, mum of five small children. Here's Esther's perspective on praying for her terminally ill son:

*Of course I'm asking for a miracle and I won't stop asking. Whatever happens, I will need a miracle. If he is fully healed and can walk again, that will be a miracle. If he dies and I have to get up every morning and carry on with my life and bring my children up in the way God wants me to, I will need a miracle. And if he survives this next two months but continues to be disabled like before, then I will need the biggest miracle of all – to set aside my many lazy and selfish desires every single day to keep giving him the specialised care and attention he needs. He is the God of miracles. He has new ones every morning. He has given us everything we have needed in the last two years – strength to fight, peace to rest, inspiration to keep moving forward, grace to cover our mistakes, hope when things were dark – I could go on and on.*

Esther movingly expresses the truth that God is a rock in the wildest storm. Whatever happens, we need his miraculous provision to carry on.[13]

## THE HEALING PLACE

My friend Joe recently asked for prayer for healing because of his crippling arthritis. Afterwards he felt peaceful but the next day the symptoms returned full force. On top of that, his mind was filled with disturbing memories and emotions. Joe's minister explained that God was answering prayer by highlighting unhealed areas that needed attention.

Joe now has a choice. He can stay where he is or travel with God. God is clearly saying 'yes' to healing Joe's emotions, memories, relationships and spiritual life. Healing his arthritis may be part of the package.

I hope and pray that it will be a complete healing for Joe; but any healing is worth having. I'd rather have a healed heart in a sick body than carry both burdens at once.

Here are some easy exercises that I use to enter the place of healing and surrender:

* Read the story of the woman healed of a haemorrhage in Mark 5:21–34. Now take hold of the bedclothes or the hem of your clothes. Imagine you're there, touching the hem of Jesus' robe. What will you ask or say?

* Imagine an empty plate and a full plate. The full plate is your situation. As you reflect on your plateful, every time you see something that hurts, move it over onto the empty plate. Everything on that plate belongs to God, so try not to steal things back. Haven't you got enough on your plate?

* If you find yourself thinking about something painful, ask God to help you face this area now. Allow your thoughts and feelings to flow. Ask God to show you anything you need to know or do. Then ask him to do what you cannot do for yourself.

---

[13] Excerpt from www.fullhands.blogspot.co.uk used by kind permission.

* Use your body. If you're able, kneeling or lying face down as you pray expresses obedience and openness to God. Holding out open hands to God is another possibility. Speak out your needs, or write them down and lay the list before God.

* Rest, listening to Christian music that you enjoy. Allow the truths in the lyrics to soak into you, like a soldier who soaks clean his battle wounds. As hurts float to the surface, release them to God.

* Pray this prayer: Lord, you see me as I am. Please receive every personal difficulty that I'm able to release to you now. Please fill me with good things. Thank you. Amen.

## *For reflection*

**1** Do you think that God still heals today?

**2** Do you have unanswered questions or hurts about healing? Is it worth checking to see if you've allowed any lies to take root in this sensitive area? To do this, pause for reflection. Any thought that opposes God's word can be weeded out repeatedly till it gives up. Seal the deal by speaking out the truth.

**3** Think of a time when your body or mind healed itself and give thanks to God for your inbuilt healing capacity. Ask God to strengthen this ability now you're ill.

**4** Can you identify layers of hurt on your particular gobstopper? Do you think God wants to heal these hurts? What factors might prevent him?

*Thank you Lord that Emily is going to have a good week, because she's going to lean on you.*

A PRAYER THAT CHANGED MY LIFE, SPOKEN BY A
YOUNG, SEVERELY DISABLED WOMAN

*A man without mirth is a like a wagon without springs. He is jolted disagreeably by every pebble in the road.*

HENRY WARD BEECHER

*If you won't feel it, God can't heal it.*

ANON

*In a futile attempt to erase our past, we deprive the community of our healing gift. If we conceal our wounds out of fear and shame, our inner darkness can neither be illuminated nor become a light for others.*

BRENNAN MANNING, *Abba's Child: The Cry of the Heart for Intimate Belonging (NavPress 2002)*

# THE MOVE
# IS ON

In the next part of Joseph's story, we're focussing on moving; moving on and moving up. I've often felt stuck in my life as a sick person, like poor jail-bound Joseph. But God is always on the move and he wants us to come too. I want to run after this dynamic God, whatever my circumstances.

## DREAMS AND MIRACLES

### GENESIS 40:1–22

Joseph was held in the royal prison. So when the king imprisoned two of his servants, Joseph was there to serve them. Then the two men had significant dreams. In Egypt, dream interpretation was left to the professionals, so there was nobody available to consult. Joseph kindly responded to their concerns and interpreted their dreams (Genesis 40:12–13, 18–19).

I love the way Joseph is learning and maturing. As a teen he boasted about his dreams, ignoring the effect on others. Now he's humble enough to grasp that God alone holds the answers, and prepared to serve freely without bitterness. Joseph's only request is that when the royal cupbearer is free, he'll try to get Joseph released. Now there's a man who believes in his own prophetic predictions!

### The big moment arrives

#### GENESIS 40:22–41:40

Joseph's words came true: the baker was executed and the cupbearer was released. Tragically, the cupbearer went on his way and forgot about helping Joseph. Joseph was left behind in prison. He must have been severely tempted to despair as the months and years dragged by. But things were just about to change.

Over in the palace, Pharaoh's mysterious dreams finally reminded the cupbearer of Joseph's talents. Joseph was fetched from the prison, scrubbed up and presented at court that very day. There was no time to go on a retreat and sort out his attitudes. Joseph was ready because he'd learned to choose God's path every day, come what may.

So here was Joseph's one big chance. Yet he made no claims for himself but offered to seek God instead. He gave Pharaoh his best shot, following up God's words with sound advice to avert the crisis to come. Joseph made a huge impact. In fact, he went from a prison cell to a Prime Minister's office in one startling day.

I'm deeply encouraged that nothing and nobody could stop Joseph. He was walking faithfully with God and so he reached his destiny.

### Fame and fortune

*So Pharaoh said to Joseph, 'I hereby put you in charge of the whole land of Egypt.' Then Pharaoh took his signet ring from his finger and put it on Joseph's finger. He dressed him in robes of fine linen and put a gold chain around his neck. He had him ride in a chariot as his second-in-command, and people shouted before him, 'Make way!' Thus he put him in charge of the whole land of Egypt.*

GENESIS 41:41–43

And so Joseph landed his dream job – leading a nation. But he was still a slave, without rights or choices. Pharaoh changed Joseph's name and married him off to a local priest's daughter. His identity and faith were in danger of being absorbed into another culture. Although his new life was much better, he had swapped one set of limits for another. Meanwhile, Joseph faced huge responsibility. He coped by using his skills and life experience, sure that God was with him.

Choice time again: Joseph could have become pleasure seeking and corrupt. He could have taken on his wife's religion and blended in with the crowd. He could have slid into bitterness: 'Will I never be free, or see my home again?'

His unseen choices at this time are shown in the meaningful names he picked for his sons (vv 51–52). His first child's name, Manasseh, means 'forget', revealing Joseph's decision to move on from sad times. Calling his second son Ephraim, which means 'twice fruitful', expressed Joseph's gratitude to God and God's ways in the face of trouble. Joseph didn't pretend things were hunky-dory but he was willing to walk with God in this new life season. That's an attitude I can admire.

## TIME TO MOVE ON

Joseph's life choices at this point strike a chord with me, even though he's a Bible superhero and I'm just me. In time, I too reached a new stage in my thinking. My agonised wails of 'Why me?' started to fade; new questions

*"Come on love, time to get up. I'll help you get dressed."*

bubbled up like fresh spring water. How can I tackle this? How can I survive day by day? What has God planned for me? This is when hope and creativity started to return.

So I was ready to get moving, although I still felt sad, ill and stressed. But just as I came out of the worst of my grief, I got bogged down in a squelchy swamp called 'I wish'.

Swampy thoughts look like this: *I wish* I could walk freely/sleep well/ stop hurting/think straight. *I wish* is a natural human reaction to loss. It's a sad sigh of the past, passivity, limitations and longings. *I wish* works hand in hand with the gloopy soup of self-pity.

Slowly I realised that I was stuck fast. It was time to stomp my way out of the swamp. The route back to solid ground was straight, if a bit steep. When a passive *I wish* thought popped up, I chose to replace it with an active *I will* thought. This moved the focus away from what I can't control to what I can work on here and now. *I will* search out ways to cope better with this symptom. *I will* find ways around this glitch. *I will* trust God even though it seems pointless. *I will*, somehow, choose to keep moving.

I find that putting on my superhero cape and making these hard choices has got a little easier with practice. And anything's better than droopy, gloopy self-pity and endless grief.

## Measuring up

My next pitfall was labelled 'I'm no good'. It's discouraging to compare today's tiny plans with what I used to do. Watching others zipping freely along their chosen path is hard, too.

It's tempting to withdraw but that's a dead end. We're all built to connect with and serve others, so we need to find a way to deal with our differences.

Paul gives wise advice on this area of comparing and competing:

> If anyone thinks they are something when they are not, they deceive themselves. Each one should test their own actions. Then they can take pride in themselves alone, without comparing themselves to someone else, for each one should carry their own load.

GALATIANS 6:3–5

Paul says I should work at meeting my own daily challenges, not peek over the fence at my past or my neighbour.

It takes practice to break the habit of comparison, but the results go wider than illness management. I can stop anxiously calculating my ranking in some imaginary league table. Instead I'm free to face my weaknesses, look to my perfect God and relax into his acceptance. 'I'm no good' is replaced with 'I'm doing my best, with God's help'.

There's a pattern to these struggles. 'Why me?', 'I wish' and 'I'm no good' are negative, passive statements. 'How?', 'I will' and 'I'm doing my best' are positive, active statements. Changing my thought patterns lifted the sad shroud of helplessness and turned my gaze outwards.

## PROBLEM SOLVING

So my thinking gradually became more active and positive. But when I looked at my situation, there were still lots of problems and challenges all around me. I needed to find a way to get on top of these problems, instead of lying down under the load.

One day I realised a simple truth. Problems need solutions – and if I can find those solutions, I can change my life. That's when things started to improve. Problem solving proved to be a great way to regain the upper hand.

I started the process by playing to my strengths. I'm a creative type, so I let my mind roam over my problem as I lay in bed. If you're less creative but quite sociable, ask someone you know or find an Internet forum. Or if you like finding things out, look around at suitable books or websites. Remember to pray and listen hard for the answer. God is interested in the challenges we face.

### Steps to success

Sometimes a problem seems too big to face. It helps to break it down into smaller steps. Think about and write down possibilities for each step:

* identify your problem

* decide on a sensible goal – you can always upgrade later
* seek out ideas to get you moving
* pick one option to try
* make a specific, reasonable short term plan
* carry out your plan, giving it time to work; expect the transition to be challenging
* check the results
* make changes if you need to, then carry out the changes and check results again
* celebrate progress, however small

If you work through these steps without results, you could try another option, ask for advice, take a rest or work on another issue. Not all problems are 100% solvable but there's usually some way to improve things.

## WHO DO YOU THINK YOU ARE?

Problem solving has an exciting hidden benefit. At first, it's restricted to tackling your own difficulties. But in the process you learn about your gifts and build your strengths. This new knowledge and experience then equips you to reach beyond yourself, to bless others.

You can make the most of this opportunity by adding self-knowledge to what you've learned so far. Think carefully about the way you tick. Ask people what you're good at. If you're well enough, you could take a personality test. Find a free test online or in a library book, or invest in a consultation.

So, who are you? Are you organised, caring, decisive, creative, determined? Are you good with children, people in crisis, animals, colour schemes, sports or numbers? Do you love to help people, pray, sing, explain things, work in a team, or meet new people? Are there things you know are not your scene?

Now add in the things you've always longed to do or change. If you don't know what your calling or your dreams are, ask God to show you and watch out for clues.

Now you're ill, of course things have changed. Some of your previous interests might seem immature or self-centred, although the underlying themes are worth a look. Other passions remain unchanged, even if you can't express them, because they're truly God-given.

Life won't be the same, because you're not the same. But life could still bring satisfying and useful moments that express your calling. Since you have tight limits, priorities have to be considered. This means that every action can count towards your goal.

## How does it work?

Let's say you feel called to creative arts, like me, and now you're too ill to lift a finger. It hurts, but your creativity will come in very handy as you tackle daily challenges and barriers. You can apply your strengths to find ways to express your calling. It's the same process as problem solving but applied to your dreams. Here are three examples to get you thinking;

* I've always loved sacred dance. When dancing wasn't possible, I found I could take part by praying for performers and later by designing and making costumes. Later, I discovered that writing was another creative outlet that suited my energy levels.
* An organised person who loves football might learn to coach, help to arrange local league fixtures or get friends together to watch the final.
* If you're interested in other countries, could you sponsor a child and find out about their culture? Could you welcome a foreign student into your home, write to a missionary abroad, sponsor a child or offer a 'conversation date' to a newly arrived neighbour with little English? How about exploring foreign cuisine, watching a suitable documentary or learning a new language?

## Learning to serve

The next stage is learning to manage your calling. It's not an excuse to throw pacing to the winds, as I discovered when I started writing my first book. I became exhausted and then confused, because I knew God was in it. Finally I realised I had to listen to God and learn how to make room for his work. I had to balance living by faith with careful attention to detail, building on what I already knew about the way I work best. I developed a regular rhythm of work, persevered despite setbacks and gave my writing high priority. Three years later, my illness was stable and my book was in the bookshops.

> *For we do not have a high priest who is unable to feel sympathy for our weaknesses, but we have one who has been tempted in every way, just as we are – yet he did not sin. Let us then approach God's throne of grace with confidence, so that we may receive mercy and find grace to help us in our time of need.*

HEBREWS 4:15–16

We're not alone with our challenges. Jesus has lived on earth and is now our representative in heaven. He understands what we are up against and is interceding for us every day. When the task is daunting, we can go confidently to ask for God's help.

## PART OF SOMETHING BIGGER

God offers suitable job opportunities to every single one of his people. The Bible tells me that Paul was called to live out God's purpose through preaching to the Gentiles. Joseph ran a famine relief programme. Deborah judged a nation. Skilled craftsmen built and decorated the Temple; many years later, a poor widow gave two copper coins for its upkeep. These familiar stories remind us that we all have unique roles to play.

Although you and I are sick, he still has significant things for us to do. How about showing perseverance through trouble? How about loving my neighbour, encouraging the weak, praying faithfully, creating beauty and order, planning something useful or sharing the Gospel? Remember, God entrusts each of us with a calling and He always offers opportunities to train for the job.

*There are different kinds of gifts, but the same Spirit distributes them. There are different kinds of service, but the same Lord. There are different kinds of working, but in all of them and in everyone it is the same God at work..*

1 CORINTHIANS 12:4–6

The chapter goes on to explain that Christians are part of the body of Christ. Each body part is dependent on all the others. I may be a hidden part but if I'm not working, the whole body is deeply affected. So my tiny contribution is still worthwhile.

## *For reflection*

**1** If you knew you'd get completely better in a month's time, would you do anything differently now? Would your prayers change?

**2** What's the problem you'd most like to solve? Start a step-by-step plan so you can work on a solution.

**3** What skills and strengths do you have to apply to fulfilling your dreams?

**4** Think about one small step in the direction of your dreams that you could take this week.

*Prayer is about getting God's will done on earth, not about getting man's will done in Heaven.*

E. M. BOUNDS

*If you think you're too small to make a difference, you've never spent the night with a mosquito.*

AFRICAN PROVERB

*Be yourself; everyone else is already taken.*

OSCAR WILDE

*All labour that uplifts humanity has dignity and importance and should be undertaken with painstaking excellence.*

MARTIN LUTHER KING JR

# FRIENDS IN THE STORM

*So the chief cupbearer told Joseph his dream ... 'This is what it means,' Joseph said ... 'But when all goes well with you, remember me and show me kindness; mention me to Pharaoh and get me out of this prison.' ... The chief cupbearer, however, did not remember Joseph; he forgot him.*

GENESIS 40:9–23

I find this part of Joseph's story almost unbearably sad. When the cupbearer was freed, he forgot all about Joseph. So Joseph was left behind in prison while his 'friend' enjoyed himself without looking back.

Many sick people hit the same problem. We're out of sight, easily overlooked, and our suffering is uncomfortable for others. So we get left out. For us, like Joseph, this casual neglect feels more like betrayal.

Relationships always change when major illness strikes. Some friends seem to expect me to take the lead in managing this change. This reminds me of the newly widowed woman who finds the neighbours crossing the road to avoid having to speak to her. It's totally unfair – but that's the way it is. I've probably done the same thing myself.

At these times, I have a difficult choice to make. I can give way to anger, hurt and despair, and sometimes I do. Or I can choose to take action over things I can control, like my own thoughts and actions. For a start, I can try to understand the other person's point of view.

## WHAT'S GOING ON?

Why do people hide just when I need them? My friend, let's call him Ben, is upset for me and upset by my illness. Ben has feelings of survivor guilt; 'I'm well and she's ill!' He doesn't know what to say and fears he might upset me.

Ben's life has changed too. He's lost the support, companionship and fun I offered in the past, so he must grieve his losses. These days, I need extra support and reassurance from Ben. He begins to feel drained, trapped and guilty. He knows he shouldn't feel sorry for himself when I am so much worse off. Ben's situation is easier than mine but it's still not easy. This complicated discomfort forces Ben to change or withdraw. He may have other major challenges right now and feel he can't carry my burdens as well.

When people disappear as trouble hits, it's very painful. Some who stay are great in the short term and others do better over a longer period. Then again, some help cheerfully with practical tasks but shy away from offering emotional support, or the other way around. It helps me to focus on enjoying what people do, rather than their shortcomings.

Major illness sparks fast personal growth. A few trusty friends are willing to travel with me and learn along the way. Others stay behind in their comfort zones, so over time we have less in common.

Of course, new friends may come along. There's nothing like talking to someone who really understands. A patient support group, newsletter or Internet forum can be a great asset. Other sufferers offer a place to discuss the details of your illness, which takes the pressure off well friends. The best support groups break isolation, boost morale and offer useful information. The worst are competitive pity parties, so watch out.

### Home alone

I find that some friends don't phone or visit, yet make time to see mutual friends who are well. This is partly because social lives are built on proximity. In other words, people go on seeing the people they see. Also, people tend to stop inviting guests who rarely show up. Perhaps they think it's sad for me to have to decline the invitation, or that it's pointless to offer.

All this is human nature, not a conspiracy against the sick. I tell my friends that I always enjoy an invitation, even if I can't go. And I try to keep in touch however I can.

Sometimes a friend says, 'Let's get together some time' and then it never happens. This is normal behaviour for a busy person but it leaves me disappointed. I've learned to say, 'What a good idea. Let's make a date now,' or I ring up later and suggest a time. It takes two to build a friendship, even if I'm the one that's ill.

## SPEAK UP

It pays to explain what's going on. If I don't say, they can't guess. Misunderstanding and hurt can finish valuable friendships. I (or a helper) could explain when is a good time to phone or visit, or explain my current limits. E-mails work well when talking is too hard.

When people say, 'If there's anything I can do . . .' I take them at their word. If I don't have an immediate suggestion, I reply, 'Thanks, that's very kind of you. Can I put your name on my helper list and let you know if I need something? No pressure if it doesn't suit.' Then I use my list when I have a specific need. I pick a small errand to start with, so a new helper won't feel swamped.

Sometimes when I ask a friend how she is, she feels guilty: 'Oh, I shouldn't complain, it's just a small thing when I look at what you're going through.' I've learned to offer this response, 'Suffering is not a competition. Your concerns matter too. I'd love to hear about you as a change from my own stuff.'

I *need* to hear these things. I'd rather feel a bit burdened than left out of the loop. This is not the same as endlessly listening to draining, negative individuals. It's about connecting genuinely with my friends when they hit a glitch.

### The prayer problem

Some less mature Christians spot my wheel chair and feel threatened by my suffering. They want to 'tidy me up' to ease their own discomfort. Or they want to see God heal through them. This type is often keen to pray for me and sometimes I agree. But if there are no apparent results, they feel the need to come up with a reason for their 'failure'. (Clue: it's a mystery!)

All this can lead to truly silly, unkind or judgmental comments. I find the only solution is to take these experiences straight to God for his comfort and wisdom. I'll be more discerning about who prays over me next time round. I'm sick but I still have the right to personal boundaries.

Caring Christian friends may also feel discouraged and unsettled if they pray for my healing and I remain sick. I'd rather hide under the duvet but they deserve some credit for trying to help. Or sometimes they want to persist in prayer, even when I've had enough. I feel like saying to them, 'Please don't offer again until you've figured out why I didn't get healed the last time you prayed!' But here are some ideas for things to say at times like that.

* Thanks for trying.
* I enjoy your company but I don't want more healing prayer at this point.
* Please pray for me to have strength to bear the burden.
* I'd find it easier if you prayed for me in my absence.

Taking an active approach relieves unwanted pressure on me. It also offers my friends clear direction and a fine learning opportunity.

## A LINE IN THE SAND

My elderly neighbour was taken away by ambulance one morning when her schizophrenia flared up. As I discussed it with another neighbour later in the day, she folded her arms and pronounced her verdict, 'The trouble with these people is they never take their medication.'

I was shocked by her harsh words but there's a reason why she appeared so uncaring. Psychologists describe a process called magic thinking, which explains why some people are so judgmental. It's like drawing a line in the sand, with the sick or suffering person on one side and the well person safely standing on the other side.

Let's say Sophie falls ill. Her friend Fred thinks, 'If she suffers, I could suffer too.' Of course anybody can suffer but we try not to think about it. So Fred starts to feel resentful towards Sophie for making him face the scary truth. He avoids Sophie, or he decides that he's different and so he's safe from her troubles. Believe me, Christians are not immune from this strange subconscious process.

'Line in the sand' thoughts look like this:

### Fred's thoughts about himself:

*I take my vitamins, so I won't get ill.*
*I exercise and eat well.*
*I'm a naturally healthy person.*

"*The problem with him is he should just get up.*"

*My family always live long lives.*
*I'm close to God – I pray for protection, so I'll be fine.*

**Fred's thoughts about Sophie:**

*She didn't look after herself.*
*Of course, if she lies in bed she will feel weak.*
*She won't follow the cure I found on the Internet.*
*The trouble with these people is they never take their medication.*
*She has no motivation to get better.*
*Illness runs in that family.*
*She doesn't believe that God will heal her – I prayed in faith, so*
*it must be her.*

Of course these ideas are nonsense. But subconscious thoughts and feelings can be extremely powerful. Because they go unnoticed, it's hard to challenge or change them.

I find this explanation very helpful. I can see why people might be afraid of my illness. Their fear speaks in words that appear spiteful, negative, judgemental, superior, rude or just plain stupid. This understanding has helped me to preserve relationships and keep my manners more or less intact in the face of some sharp testing.

### Miracle cures

There's a 21st-century pitfall here, so watch your footing. You may find yourself bombarded with information on Internet miracle cures. Each supporter is convinced he's found just what you need. Friends can feel aggrieved if you don't choose to take 'their' cure. It's another hill to climb, risking emotional pressure, judgment or rejection from those around you.

I'm at the point where I dread the next announcement of someone's pet cure for ME. It's hard to explain to my well friend why I'm not instantly thrilled to hear it and it's hard to see the disappointment in her eyes. This is heavy stuff, leaving me drained and deflated every time.

It's not safe or wise to give your health management over to a self-appointed 'expert' committee. You can deflect friendly fire by thanking supporters for their concern, saying it's good to have a range of treatments to explore when you feel ready. This shows that you're the one in the driving seat.

It's worth finding out what lies behind an alternative therapy before diving in. Some 'cures' are useful and life giving. Some are based on other faiths or occult belief systems and may bring spiritual bondage in their wake. Some are a waste of time and money and a few may do physical harm. Taking time to find out more will help you make a wise decision.

## HONESTY *v* 'PASSING FOR NORMAL'

Bob and Charles share a long term interest in Japan. After much prayer, they decided to fly to Japan for a short missions trip. Bob suffers from depression. After three hectic days in Japan, he needed a day in bed to recover. At this point Charles got annoyed. 'Why didn't you tell me you needed so much rest? I need your help today.' Bob explained that with his depression, he often needs extra rest. Charles retorted that Bob should have been honest about this before they left. Then Charles stomped out, leaving Bob stuck in a pit with no warning.

The problem is that Bob has learned to spare his well friends from the realities of his illness. He prefers not to dwell on his illness. He also fears that people might reject him if they know how ill he is. So he rests up before and after social events, hides when he feels lousy and makes light of his symptoms to others. Sadly, Bob's well-meaning strategy misled Charles into thinking that Bob's illness is not too bad.

Like Bob, I try to play down my struggles to keep my friends. I complain that nobody understands what I'm going through – but then I hide my illness away. It seems I'm always after something: a lift, wheelchair access, a listening ear, wheat free food or an early night. I want to share my life with others but I don't want to put anybody off. It feels like I'm endlessly performing, hoping well people will choose to put up with me. The power balance is askew.

The effect is to undermine my confidence and erode my sense of self. Fear of rejection drags me down when I could be having fun. I feel diminished and substandard but God's word says my value is secure.

So the first step out of this pit is to repair my identity by drawing close to God. I need to take time to soak up his words of love for me. The next step is to get creative and start to serve as God directs. Even tiny actions can encourage others, boost my self-esteem and improve that wonky power balance.

### Good to go

So what has a sick person got to offer a well friend? The key is to use whatever you have:

* Time – offer to listen, pray over an issue, look online for something, problem solve, babysit, bake, seek out a suitable joke or quotation, offer a lift, find or make a thoughtful and affordable gift.
* A stable home base – take in a parcel, host an overnight guest or be a phone or e-mail contact for an event.

* An uncluttered diary – buy a supply of cards and mark in all those birthdays, anniversaries and exam dates, with a week's grace to get them to the post on time.
* Love – show your friends they matter to you by listening and responding thoughtfully.

A relative of mine was off work recently, recovering from exploratory cancer surgery. He posted me some useful information that he found during a clearout. I deeply appreciate the way he thought of me during his time of crisis. I hope my friends will receive my small offerings in the same spirit.

## JOINED TO OTHERS

In this season of illness, God offers a new opportunity to develop compassion. I find there's nothing like struggle, failure, frustration and tears to help me spot others who are hurting. Paul offers wise advice about truly caring for others: 'Rejoice with those who rejoice; mourn with those who mourn.' (Romans 12:15)

I often find it difficult to rise above my own sufferings. But this is God's life-giving word, so obedience carries a blessing. When I make the effort to mourn or rejoice with others, I remember that I'm not the only one who suffers. I can rejoin my community by offering sympathy, attention and enthusiasm to others.

Likewise, I've learned to connect myself with life events. I can ask for the date and time of that vital exam, job interview or hospital appointment. I offer to pray and put the details in my diary to remind me. Later I ask after the results, which means I stay in the story.

Even when things are particularly challenging, it brightens up my day to see another person's joy. Small triumphs are doubled as I enter in to my friend's pleasure with a sincere heart. This is fun for both of us, not a noble service I offer through gritted teeth. Well, sometimes I start with gritted teeth but my emotions naturally follow my choices. A smile is usually the end result.

Those who find it difficult socially, or are tucked away in bed, can still care for others. Make contact with reputable charities, individuals or groups who serve others. Do what you can to enter in: pray, give, offer encouragement, lobby, sign a petition, find out more. This offers a connection to someone else's situation, wherever and whoever they are.

Even the very poorly can watch out for opportunities to encourage or ask after someone: friends, carers, neighbours, relatives or fellow patients. Your caring attitude, acceptance and concern could make all the difference to someone you see. Small offerings to others make a big impact when God gets involved. And part of that impact rebounds to bless you, too.

## For reflection

**1** Have any of your relationships changed because of your illness?

**2** Have you had any 'line in the sand' comments from others?

**3** Write and send a short note of thanks to someone who's helped you lately.

*It makes no sense to try to extend a friendship that was only meant to be a season into a lifetime.*

MANDY HALE

*There is nothing better than a friend, unless it is a friend with chocolate.*

LINDA GRAYSON

*Animals are such agreeable friends – they ask no questions, they pass no criticisms.*

GEORGE ELIOT

# SINGLE AND SICK

Singleness plus sickness is tough. This calls for a heavy-duty Bible hero to look up to. Since Joseph eventually married, for this chapter we'll focus on Daniel.

In the beginning, Daniel had it all. He was young, good-looking, healthy, high born, intelligent and well educated. Then his country was invaded by Babylonian forces. Daniel and his mates were captured and taken away to lifelong slavery.

Daniel is usually portrayed as a hunky action man, standing tall with clenched fists, a rippling robe and a six-pack. But the truth is rather different. The Babylonian custom was to castrate male slaves after they were captured in battle. After the initial pain, fear and humiliation, other changes would follow. Over the months voices rose, muscles dwindled and bodies softened with new fat distribution. Sex drive diminished, mood swings began and shaving ceased. Marriage and children were now impossible. And there was no privacy as they grieved over losing their manhood.

## Choice time

Next, the young men were enrolled onto a three-year course in Babylonian Studies. Just like Joseph in Egypt, their names were changed and they were expected to immerse themselves in local culture. Because they were on a fast-track to royal service, there was a student perk. They were fed good food and fine wine from the king's kitchen. The drawback was that the food was not permitted for Jewish believers.

Now Daniel was a long way from home. Nobody was there to blame him for eating delicious, nourishing food. A spot of comfort eating seems like a harmless way to regain a bit of happiness in a very bleak life season. On top of that, as a slave he risked severe punishment for making any comment or complaint. He must have thought very carefully before asking permission to stop eating the king's food.

The story shows that Daniel took the hard choice and that God blessed him for it. This pattern of faith, integrity and provision repeats itself throughout this fascinating Bible book. Daniel never made it home to freedom. But God used him powerfully over many years, because Daniel was committed to God. He may not have been a hunk but he's still my hero.

## CLOSER TO HOME

I'll come clean. I've never been single and sick. I can't say I fancy it, either. I have some wonderful single sick friends who I deeply respect. Here's what they tell me they're facing:

### Romantic issues

* trouble meeting a partner
* being too ill for a relationship
* a ticking biological clock
* sexual frustration
* no stable, dependable relationship

### Personal issues

* money worries
* housing uncertainties
* having nobody around for company, entertainment, support, care
* fear of the future
* loneliness
* social expectation to care for elderly relatives
* not enough hugs
* not fitting in to their age group as time goes by
* casual discrimination against singles
* social isolation

* the pain of uncertainty
* maintaining faith while handling ongoing loss
* feeling left out and diminished

James feels his illness and treatment has directly impacted his social life:

> *I suffer from social anxiety as well as schizophrenia. Also, when I was young, my church had strict teaching against TV, going to the pub or parties. So I became isolated when I needed practice with socialising.*
>
> *I wonder if I will ever have proper relationships again, especially marriage. I am getting older than my years and I have a very poor track record with work. My medication has caused me to be overweight, too.*

James carries the extra burden of uncertainty.[14] He might find someone special, and he might not. Nobody can reassure him about his future, which adds to his struggles now.

This stuff is really hard, on top of the illness issues we all face. Where do single believers find strength?

Sally comments:

> *It's a struggle. But my confidence comes from God and I would want that whether I was sick or well. Being single FORCES me to look to God for these things. There isn't that special someone in my life, loving me and caring for me and giving me confidence. So maybe it is not all bad. I can't rely on another person because there isn't one in my life.*
>
> *It is difficult at times to relate to and be included in the world. People exclude you as you are not part of a couple. I often feel you have to try harder to maintain social contact and make sure you are invited to things. And it's harder to go alone to gatherings. Being sick adds that extra difficulty and limitation but it's hard to be single, regardless of your health. Other single friends are a lifeline, whether healthy or sick. The issues you face are the same and you can support each other.*

Sally sees the value of building a network of people who can offer support in different ways. But as she's discovered, this priority also leads to hard choices:

> *When you only have a tiny amount of energy, it's very difficult to meet potential partners. Most of the time, to my mind, it simply isn't worth using that precious energy to try and connect with strangers rather than precious friends/family. If God has someone for me, my illness and limitations aren't going to stop him bringing that person into my life.*
>
> *Sometimes I think I feel less pressure than my healthy single friends - the 'world' assumes I am single due to my illness where as they are judged for their singleness and often feel looked down upon.*

---

[14] Look on p 64, Chapter 7, 'Finding firm footing' for more about handling uncertainty.

Sally's comments make me see that our culture is built by and for the comfortably married. How shallow and unfair to judge single people because of their personal losses or choices. The church is not immune, often leaving singles out in the cold when it comes to leadership opportunities or social occasions. This is a loss for us all.

It strikes me that Daniel's castration meant he was excluded from priesthood back home. Yet God used Daniel's wise and uncompromising words to change the nation of Babylon, time after time. It seems that God is less interested in marital status than what's in a person's heart.

## WHO AM I?

Since my friend started training to be a counsellor, I've noticed that things have changed. He asks, 'Why?' a lot and tends to lean back and look carefully at me when I speak. Weird counselling jargon also appears when it's least expected. The other day he said, 'I'm trying to get better at being me.'

Apparently, this is classic 'counsel-speak' but I like this idea. In a culture that dictates how we should look, sound, behave, dress and think, it's easy to lose the plot. Ill and isolated, we end up striving to reach a flawed version of perfection, or losing the sense of being a Proper Person.

Asking 'Who am I?' and 'How can I get better at being me?' will help me become more like Jesus. God has unique plans for each person, so he made me distinctive and special. If I waste my time trying to be someone else, I end up bland and boring, like a beige carpet.

On the other hand, becoming more like Jesus is neither easy nor comfortable. But it means I become more like my authentic, colourful self. That's a worthwhile goal.

## *For reflection*

**1** Do you view Daniel any differently, now you know what he lost?

**2** For you, what's the worst bit of being single? What's the best bit?

**3** Try displaying something personal and precious in your home. What does it say about you?

*Let not our longing slay the appetite of our living.*
JIM ELLIOTT

*'If you fall, I'll be there.' Signed, The Floor*
ANON

*'Oh, Lizzy! do anything rather than marry without affection.'*
JANE AUSTEN, *Pride and Prejudice*

*Before you start to judge me, step into my shoes and live the life I'm living, and maybe, just maybe, you will see how strong I really am.*
ANON

*I'm single because I was born that way.*
MAE WEST

*I was regretting the past, and fearing the future. Suddenly, my Lord was speaking: 'My name is not I WAS; When you live in the future with its problems and fears it is hard, I am not there, for my name is not I WILL BE. When you live in this moment it is not hard, I am here, for my name is I AM'*

ANON

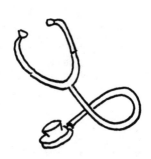

# FACING
# THE WORLD

*So the warder put Joseph in charge of all those held in the prison, and he was made responsible for all that was done there. The warder paid no attention to anything under Joseph's care, because the LORD was with Joseph and gave him success in whatever he did. ... When Joseph came to them the next morning, he saw that they were dejected. So he asked Pharaoh's officials . . . 'Why do you look so sad today?' 'We both had dreams,' they answered, 'but there is no one to interpret them.'*

*Then Joseph said to them, 'Do not interpretations belong to God? Tell me your dreams . . . But when all goes well with you, remember me and show me kindness; mention me to Pharaoh and get me out of this prison.'*

GENESIS 39:22–23, 40:6–8, 14

Have you noticed that Joseph was good with people? Even when he was powerless and poor, he had the knack of getting on with his boss. Since the sick must cooperate with others, perhaps I can learn from his approach.

This part of the story reveals that Joseph was hardworking, tactful, thoughtful towards others and humble enough to ask for help. These are all areas that a sick person is free to work on. The Lord was with Joseph to give him success and the Lord is also with us. So there's every chance to make things better.

Ill people are often up against powerful systems and individuals. We visit the doctor, apply for benefits or services and deal with carers. We try to fit in with our well friends and families. Sometimes there's discrimination or hostility to handle. This chapter looks at our interactions with powerful people.

## PART OF SOMETHING BIGGER

We all live in some kind of community. When someone falls ill it affects their place in the community, whether they like it or not.

For example, it seems that in our culture it's 'okay' to blame certain groups for their troubles, such as the overweight, smokers, benefit applicants and anybody who contracts HIV. Mental illness can give you a new outlook – the backs of your friends as they disappear over the hill. Any illness that isn't promptly diagnosed raises the risk of people not believing you. Cancer, meanwhile, gives you a new label overnight as the brave and tragic victim, distant from normal life. A set of wheels under your seat apparently transforms you into somebody else. All this is silly and tiring. 'Hello', you want to shout, 'I'm still in here!'

If you're suddenly wheeling around or your vision or hearing goes downhill, disabled access and specialist services move from the very edge of life to being totally central. This is part of the community's response to illness, along with hospital waiting lists, prescription prices, social care and benefits. Then there's that helpful shop assistant, or kids who stare at you in the street because you look different.

Of course some aspects of community response can be helpful and encouraging. I opened the door one poorly day to find a local teenager on the doorstep with a fruit flan she'd made herself. It tasted delicious and the memory of her kindness still cheers me up. Remaining part of a church gives a bright spot of normality, and any positive contact with the NHS leaves me feeling valued and respected.

When and if we're able, the sick are well placed to recycle painful experience into priceless support for others. We can offer the lifeline of understanding, adding in our concern, respect and acceptance. This kind of community, often found online these days, can be very powerful.

## FACING STRANGERS

On my first outing with my new carer Ella, she seemed to know everybody we passed. All was well until we came towards a cheery-looking older man in a checked cap. 'Hello, Ella!' said he, smiling at her while pointing

directly into my face at close quarters. 'I didn't recognise you pushing *that!*'

We let him walk on by, mostly because neither of us could find a word to say. I fought an urge to give chase, pin him to the wall with my wheelchair and list my accomplishments until he acknowledged me as a Person, not a Thing.

Another day, Ella and I were crossing the road. A young driver clearly saw us, then chose to speed up and drove right at us, laughing merrily. Ella was forced to sprint to get us to the safety of the pavement. We were left shaken and tearful.

I find it tempting to stay in when something bad happens but that's no way to go on. I've learned to put on my confidence ahead of time, like wearing armour into battle. A sense of humour adds a cosy under-layer: that's my thermal undies.

Others tend to take their cue from my body language and the way I speak to them. It helps to make friendly eye contact. People don't like to be caught staring.

This confidence took time to find. I had to get used to life on wheels and learn to agree with God's loving assessment of my value. The rest is up to others; it's not my problem. If people stare, I pretend it's because I'm famous. Rude reactions can be remembered to laugh about later.

Of course, this approach only deals with the milder stuff. Disability hate crime is thankfully now a police matter. It's worth taking yourself seriously enough to complain when something really nasty happens. It's a pity Ella and I didn't get that driver's registration number.

## FACING YOUR FRIENDS

Jenna was plunged into severe illness in her early twenties. Her active, sporty life changed to lying silently in bed, too ill to get dressed or use the phone. Jenna continued to e-mail her friends but her friend Sam didn't respond. She found this odd, as they had been quite close. One day she heard that he'd made this throwaway comment; 'Oh, Jenna, she's changed so much. She's just no fun any more.'

Handling an unpleasant stranger is hard but hurtful reactions from friends or family strike much deeper. The pain of rejection can blight relationships and erode courage and confidence. Painful feelings rapidly take root and grow into an ugly jungle.

I've found that rampant rejection can be cut right back, with a bit of smart thinking. The key is to get specific about what's happening. Here are some examples of rejected thought patterns, followed by the grain of truth in the middle.

* My family don't understand me. (Auntie Hilda thinks fresh air can cure anything, even my psychosis.)
* I'm targeted in my neighbourhood. (Two boys shouted a rude remark because I was a bit slow crossing the road.)
* I'm deformed and people stare. (I have swollen fingers and a toddler stared at them in a shop last week.)

* My church doesn't care about me. (Jo and Simon know my phone number, but they haven't rung me since my operation.)
* My sister hates me now I'm ill. (My sister is critical of everybody she knows.)

Hmm. Looks a bit different, doesn't it?

Now to attack the roots of rejection. At the risk of repetition, why should I allow others to judge my worth? That's God's job. My job is to accept his valuation and live in the good of it. Here are some wise words from Henri Nouwen:

> *As soon as someone accuses me or criticises me, as soon as I am rejected, left alone, or abandoned, I find myself thinking, 'Well, that proves once again that I am a nobody.' ... [My dark side says,] I am no good ... I deserve to be pushed aside, forgotten, rejected, and abandoned. Self-rejection is the greatest enemy of the spiritual life because it contradicts the sacred voice that calls us the 'Beloved.' Being the Beloved constitutes the core truth of our existence.'*

So I need to feed my heart with God's love and acceptance to help me hold my head high. On the back of that, it may be time to attend to other areas. I might need to do some more grieving, work on rebuilding my fragile self-esteem or take time to care for my needs. It helps me to keep a healthy focus when I find things I like to do and plan to do them.

Rejection shuts out the light, creating and then feeding on a very narrow perspective. One way to break out of this restricted mindset is to talk to someone you trust. If you're very isolated, talking to a counsellor or minister might offer you a fresh point of view.

## FACING YOUR CARER

Being ill alters the balance of power. This unseen issue can drag down caring relationships. For example, sometimes I feel helpless, like a child, because of my dependence. This dependence can be financial, practical or emotional, depending on the situation. My carer or helper might feel guilty, overburdened or unable to say no. It's frustrating and draining all round. If things aren't going well, here are some suggestions:

* Talk through your own feelings with another person first.
* Discuss the issues calmly with your carer, choosing a good time for both parties. Explain how specific things make you feel and ask if the other person has difficulties too. Perhaps you can find a solution together, or suggest one of your own.
* Make sure your carer has time off to lessen the intensity of your time together.
* Try to spot and defuse manipulation, be it theirs or yours.

If you feel bullied, threatened or controlled by your carer, please talk to someone soon. It could be a relative, a doctor or minister. There may be aspects that can be resolved, or it may be time to look for a change of scene.

From your end, manipulation is a classic human reaction to powerlessness. It's very tempting to set up a request so it's hard to refuse but the payback is toxic and long-lasting. If people feel manipulated they will withdraw, either emotionally or practically. If the only way to get what you need is to put unfair pressure on others, it's time to reassess your care needs and make a new plan.

## FACING YOUR DOCTOR

The traditional doctor-patient relationship has the doctor speaking, acting and deciding, while the patient nods, hands folded meekly in her lap. Thankfully, things have changed in the years since I did my training. You could think of your doctor as a 'human repairs and maintenance' technician. You need the technical input but you are the owner of the body and central to the healing process.

Most doctors are hoping for a patient who speaks up, explains what's going on and asks what they need to know. Doctors are not mind readers, after all. They're pushed for time, so if you can sort out what you want to say and ask beforehand, you'll get more out of a short consultation. Taking notes, or asking your doctor to write down a crucial point, helps you retain the information. A companion can also be helpful in making sure things get said and facts are remembered. Following up new information afterwards will give you the best results.

Becoming a well-informed patient who actively participates in your own health care gives you a better chance of recovery. As a bonus, you're saved from feeling like a passive victim who's kept in the dark. Mutual respect and understanding can be built over time. If there's none of that, maybe you have the wrong doctor.

In the end, you might know more about your illness than your doctor does, particularly if the illness is rare. This can be disconcerting for both of you. Turning up with several pages of information off the Internet is not helpful to a doctor who lacks time to read it. She's only human; she might feel threatened by an expert patient. She's more likely to take new ideas on board if you're pleasant and stick to the point.

> I tend to use my doctor for endless prescription requests, and collating all the paperwork from therapists, nurses and consultants, so I don't actually see him that often. I only go if there's a crisis. Trusting your instincts is very important, like when to go to the doctor and when not to, and when it might be best to change doctor. I did have a good GP but found it hard to get an appointment, so I saw a different doctor who sees a couple of my friends with many health issues. He very quickly grasped what the issues were, which helped me to trust him. My doctor can help me work out if something is a crisis or help me to monitor things. Also, don't be afraid to go to your doctor if you aren't coping with things. I had 'doctor avoidance' for years and shot myself in the foot. I learned the hard way how important it is have a good GP who you can trust.

Working with a home carer, nurse or home help can also be a challenge. The same strategies apply. Say what you want and need; try to work actively and respectfully with the professionals. Trying to DIY in the face of offered help may be misguided, because help with one thing can release energy for you to use elsewhere.

Saying 'well done' and 'thank you' go a long way to foster a good relationship with anybody, whether they wear a uniform or not.

### Wrong doctor?

If you often disagree with your doctor, feel bullied or that there's a personality clash, it's time to take action. It's worth checking out the doctor's approach first. You could ask your patient association helpline, or ask for a medical second opinion. Your doctor might be right this time, after all.

If you're still not happy, you could take a friend along for moral support and tactfully address the difficulties. If that fails, you could start seeing a different GP partner or change to another practice. I followed this process after years of difficulty. I found it helpful to face and pray over my hurt feelings when I finally left the practice. This released me to make a fresh start with my new doctor, although it took time to rebuild my confidence.

You have rights as a patient. So long as you're well enough to understand what's going on, you can say 'No,' at any point. You can refuse any treatment, investigation, hospital admission or examination.

You don't have to have medical students present at a consultation or treatment session. But if you feel able, you can help to train good doctors for the future. I really appreciate the patients who allowed me to look, listen and 'have a prod'. I still remember the lessons they taught me.

## A SAFE PLACE

When Moses was very old, he spoke blessings over the tribes of Israel as a final legacy. Benjamin's blessing speaks to me of my place in the world:

> *About Benjamin he said: 'Let the beloved of the LORD rest secure in him, for he shields him all day long, and the one the LORD loves rests between his shoulders.'*

DEUTERONOMY 33:12

For a toddler, going on Daddy's shoulders is a great treat. An adult's long strides carry him along at dizzying speed and there's a great view from up there. Best of all, Daddy is close by to ward off anything scary. My little nephew liked to steer by taking a firm grip of his Daddy's ears, which was funny to watch but hard on the ears concerned.

This image of a child sitting safely on Father God's shoulders gives me confidence when I feel daunted and small. I don't have to stand alone, overshadowed by powerful people; in truth, I'm riding high.

## *For reflection*

1 Have you ever faced discrimination, hassle or hostility from others? If so, how did you deal with it?

2 If a relative or friend cares for you, try standing in their shoes. If you were well and caring for them, how would you feel about their limits and trials? Would you enjoy caring for them? What would you have to give up to make time?

3 Write a note, text or card to say thanks for what your carer does for you, whether they are paid or unpaid. No need for an epistle.

4 How are things with your doctor? Think about thanking him/her for whatever's good or helpful. Even if other things are bad, this paves the way for negotiating change.

*Pay no attention to what the critics say; no statue has ever been erected to a critic.*

JEAN SIBELIUS, composer

*Some people think that doctors and nurses can put scrambled eggs back in the shell.*

CASS CANFIELD

*Though the doctors treated him, let his blood, and gave him medications to drink, he nevertheless recovered.*

LEO TOLSTOY, *War and Peace*

# FAMILY MATTERS

Upbringing and family life has a huge impact on the way anyone handles illness. In the other direction, illness disrupts and changes families. This chapter looks at updating family influences, handling relatives and standing your ground in an imperfect family. These themes thread right through the story of Joseph, so follow me for a quick family tour.

## SOME TRUTHS

### GENESIS 37

Joseph grew up in a messy, complicated family, a wealthy polygamous tribe with Jacob as its rather devious head. The family stories were of Uncle Laban's dodgy business dealings, Jacob's shady past, wifely in-fighting and the occasional tendency of Grandfather Abraham to lie his way out of a tight corner.

Reuben, the firstborn son, was top dog until he misbehaved and lost his birthright. After that, Jacob favoured Joseph and gave him a special robe to wear, which was a daily reminder of Jacob's choice. Joseph's brothers hated him because they were jealous, and there was also bad blood over Joseph's high standards in the family business. So young Joseph was a high achiever but short on humility, which is hardly surprising. He and his brothers had a lot to learn.

### Brotherly love

#### GENESIS 42:1–8

As we know, Joseph's brothers callously sold him off to travelling slave traders. Some twenty years later a famine hit the region, so the brothers went off to buy food from the new governor of Egypt. The scene was set for a family reunion.

Young Joseph had suffered rejection, hatred, jealousy and loss at the hands of his brothers. Twenty years later there they were, face down, begging in front of him. His dreams had come strangely true. They didn't even recognise him – but he knew them alright. Now he held absolute power over them, would he choose revenge or mercy?

### A new start

GENESIS 42:9 – 45:28

It's interesting that the pace of the story changes completely at this point, from a bare list of events to lengthy details. We hear each person's state of mind and the reasoning behind every decision. We're even shown the menu and the seating plan. This part of Joseph's story was hugely important to him and so every detail was recorded.

Back at that fateful meeting, Joseph had spent many years learning how to forgive and understand the human heart. He was ready to rebuild healthy relationships.

Joseph showed forgiveness and mercy, yet took care to avoid trouble. He tested the brothers over many weeks before finally having an emotional reunion. In a dramatic climax, Joseph wept uncontrollably as he hugged his brothers one by one. After talking long into the night, he sent them home laden with gifts to rescue the rest of the family. He even cracked a joke in parting:

> . . . and as they were leaving he said to them, 'Don't quarrel on the way!
>
> GENESIS 45:24b

### Happy ever after?

GENESIS 50:15–21

The situation was not perfect, even so. Joseph always had to be the grown-up in that family. His brothers never grew out of jealousy, distrust and manipulation, but Joseph treated them fairly and kindly till the day he died. He was truly set free from the past.

## FAMILY STYLE

Every family has a different culture, with its own traditions and strategies. Some aspects of this are likely to be helpful, others are not. Family background powerfully impacts an individual's approach to their difficulties, even in adult life.

Becky was a young mother when she slipped on a wet floor and damaged her back severely. Her reaction to her situation was definitely shaped by her background:

> I am a Jewess who found Jesus; my people get up and get on with it. This caused me to push myself too much. Also, my mother was always ill and expected to be 'waited on'. It ruined my childhood. I was not going to treat my family like that, so I did not make it easy for myself. All I did was put myself into more pain; after much prayer and ministry things have changed, but I still do not push my children or grandchildren.

Sunil avoids his family's coping style, choosing instead what he's learned as an adult believer:

> The only coping skills on offer while growing up in my family would be to take drugs or alcohol. I chose to live in a supporting community of faith, stable marriage and knowing 'God works all things together for good' as the ways to deal with trials. No way could I have dealt with this without his grace!

Sadly, family is sometimes directly linked to illness. James's family has had a lot of mental health problems. His parents met as patients in a psychiatric ward, his uncle took his own life and his brothers have both had episodes of mental illness.

This unusual background has had a big impact on James. He was always at higher risk of mental illness as an individual, because of inherited risk factors and perhaps also his upbringing. James has had to assess his family coping styles very carefully.

On the other hand, James's dad Charlie has a lot of experience with mental illness. This makes Charlie a kind and understanding supporter. James treasures the memory of Charlie's visit during a relapse:

> *I was seriously ill for the first time that winter and spent two short periods in hospital. My dad came a long way to visit me, despite the fact that he was using two walking sticks and had to crawl up the stairs to get to the flat where I was staying.*

In his turn, James tries to support his brothers if they are particularly poorly.

### Pick and mix

Closer to home, what did you learn from your upbringing? Is it all useful to you now, or is it time to reassess?

Thinking, praying and talking to others will help you understand the way you grew up. Try to make a list of family strategies, attitudes or habits and consider them one by one. Look at every aspect, good or bad. For example, I found my family's strong work ethic very useful when I was well. It became a problem when I fell ill, because I felt guilty for 'being lazy' when I paced myself properly.

Once I had decided what was worth keeping and what needed updating, I asked God to help me with the process of change. I chose a specific goal: 'I'm going to speak and think positively about myself when I'm resting, instead of believing that I'm lazy'. I try to stop and challenge myself every time I act or think in the old way.

This process gets easier with practice but it all takes time. It might help to pray with someone or perhaps have counselling, depending on the issues.

## THE CARER RELATIONSHIP

If you're blessed with family or friends who look after you, these relationships will be changed by the caring process. There are the original bonds between you, some of which remain, and others will be changed by illness. For example, Stuart and his dad enjoy going to football matches together but now Stuart can't handle crowds. They still talk about football and watch it together on TV.

As well as any changes imposed by the illness, there's the burden of your suffering and your needs to add to your relationships. Some friends or family members will bow out at this point, while others will stay the course. Either way, the relationships have to adjust. Trying to live in the past will not help anybody.

Having been on both ends of this caring business, sometimes both at once, I know that being a carer is really frustrating. Carers must try to help, with or without gratitude or understanding. When you get it wrong, you'll get told off. Even when you get it right, they'd rather do it themselves.

You live in their limited world, at their slow pace. You're pained by their suffering but you can't resolve their troubles. As their abilities and lifestyle are changed by illness, you both grieve the loss of the past.

As well as all this, caring eats up time and energy. It's no wonder a carer can end up bruised and daunted. They may feel guilty because they aren't the one who's suffering. In fact, they are suffering too, in a different way.

I felt sad and guilty while watching my family do without an active, able wife and mother. I regret the severe limits placed on my kids as they grew and also the struggle my husband and mum went through. This suffering was their life circumstances, which they had to work through under God. We all watched each other suffer.

The positive side is the great love and companionship built between the sick and those who are brave enough to truly care for them. These relationships are pure gold, refined in the fire, and clearly express the nature of God to those around. Others may have less to offer, but a well-timed word of encouragement or a spot of practical help can still be savoured.

## GROWING UP AND MOVING ON

If you've been ill since childhood, family relationships are combined with illness. There's a parent/carer or two and a child/patient. Then adolescence arrives to overturn these familiar patterns. An ill teenager needs to take over responsibility for managing his illness as well as handling the normal teenage stuff. Parents must stand back, bite their tongues and watch as their boy takes the reins. This process is difficult for all. It may remain as a family stress point long after he reaches adulthood.

Perhaps you missed the impact of your own diagnosis or other health crises because you were too young to understand. It may help to talk through what happened, asking how parents felt, accessing your old medical notes or talking to your doctor. This process helps you to settle any unspoken emotional issues. It may also help you to understand what your parents have been through and why they react the way they do, even now.

Layla was birth injured and needed a lot of care in her childhood. Other complications followed, leaving her increasingly disabled. Here she reflects on the process of leaving home:

> *My Mum and Dad have always encouraged me to 'push through things' and trust the Lord, no matter what. They could have wrapped me in cotton wool but instead allowed and even encouraged me to move away.*
>
> *I remember how lost I was when I left home at nineteen. It's been such a struggle, a fight all the way. It's a curious mixture of growing independence coupled with forced dependence.*
>
> *I'm less independent now, ten years on, because of the increased care I need. I often feel too dependent on my parents, as though I have no choice but to treat them as PAs sometimes. For example if I'm with my parents, I need help with self-care, or my flat might need to be cleaned. I hate asking my parents for help and am really bad at it.*
>
> *There are times when I just do not have the energy to keep going. I don't always feel my family understand and it can be highly frustrating. At other times they realise how restricted I am and try to help me accept it. I can find it tough relating to them as sometimes I still feel like a child.*

Some adults are too poorly to leave the family home. Others may come and go according to their state of health. This goes painfully against the natural patterns of independence, leaving the whole family stuck in a time warp. It can help to literally put away childish things, storing away books and toys and redecorating the bedroom to mark a fresh start. Talking through key issues with parents might clear the air and allow a fresh start. A thoughtful letter can be useful, or the help of a trusted 'referee'.

## STRUCK DOWN BUT NOT DESTROYED

*But we have this treasure in jars of clay to show that this all-surpassing power is from God and not from us. We are hard pressed on every side, but not crushed; perplexed, but not in despair; persecuted, but not abandoned; struck down, but not destroyed. We always carry around in our body the death of Jesus, so that the life of Jesus may also be revealed in our body.*

2 CORINTHIANS 4:7–10

In the heat of battle, it's tempting to despair. I've sometimes felt that the illness was taking everything: career, independence, the chance to serve and connect with others, quality of life, family freedoms and my future. I find the passage above very comforting at these dark times. It offers a balanced view of the unavoidable struggles of life in a fallen world.

Paul starts by putting human weakness and belief into perspective. God's glory is present in my messy, breakable life. That seems ridiculous, like carrying the Crown jewels around in a flimsy plastic bag. This stark contrast is designed to show up God's beauty and power all the more.

Next, Paul explains that my struggles will not be the end of me. Yes, I'm hard pressed and struck down – but I won't be crushed or destroyed. Remember, Paul was facing serious risk of execution and massive pressures every day. So this passage isn't offering escape from hardship. It goes far deeper than that.

As I face the daily grind of life with illness, I can rest on this mystery. My weakness has a purpose. My fragile health is like a darkly coloured picture frame that sets off God's perfection. And through God's plan, my suffering will not have the last word. God will provide what I need, come what may.

## *For reflection*

**1** What's your earliest memory?

**2** What were your family's coping styles as you grew up? Are they useful to you now?

**3** If you have a related carer, how's it going? Would it help to ask them how they feel about looking after you?

*People are pretty forgiving when it comes to other people's families. The only family that ever horrifies you is your own.*

DOUG COUPLAND

*Sooner or later we all quote our mothers.*

BERN WILLIAMS

*You don't choose your family. They are God's gift to you, as you are to them.*

DESMOND TUTU

*It was nice growing up with someone like you – someone to lean on, someone to count on … someone to tell on!*

ANON

# THREE'S A CROWD

# 17

Illness is really annoying. Like a wriggly puppy, it just won't stay put. For example, last spring my son and his partner travelled many miles to visit us. They wanted to tell us in person that they were expecting our first grandchild. During the joyful group hug that followed, I realised that I wouldn't be well enough to visit them when the baby was born. My heart sank. Even in this special moment, my illness had pushed its wet nose into the picture.

Illness has a tendency to sneak in to all areas of marriage and family life. I've gathered together every resource I can think of to help the sick build healthy households, despite all.

## A BEAR IN THE BED

Illness brings unexpected pressures into a marriage. Communication can falter as one partner sails away into unknown waters. A happy sex life is often jolted off track and the household budget takes a beating.

If things get tense, an ill husband may feel frightened of losing both his life partner and his live-in carer. Illness keeps him in, so he may not have anyone else to talk to about it. Or he may not feel well enough to cope with confronting the problems. Meanwhile his overstretched wife feels guilty for wishing things were different.

When illness moved in with us, it was like waking up to find a bear in the double bed. He was big, hairy, wedged firmly in the middle and he snored. Pillows and people were being pushed out. The whole thing was in danger of collapsing under the strain. We needed to wake up, get real and build a bigger bed.

What I mean is that these unwelcome pressures can be used to build a stronger relationship. This process needs a dose of realism, willingness to change and careful attention to daily priorities. If all that sounds too

difficult, start small. Here are three simple strategies that have helped us over the years.

### The power of speech

First of all, speak well. Here are two compliments a sick husband might offer;

* ❋ 'Thank you for driving me to the doctor's surgery. I know it's a busy day for you.'
* ❋ You're so funny. I love the way you see the brighter side.'

The first comment marks effort and offers thanks. This gives his wife a boost and feeds her motivation.

The second remark appreciates his wife for who she is, rather than what she does. It's vital for him to remember and celebrate his beloved bride. She's still there, tucked away inside the tired carer who needs a haircut. Being noticed helps his wife to feel appreciated and loved as a person.

Of course, these compliments can flow the other way, too. Sick people also have personal strengths, attitudes and achievements that are worth a round of applause.

Sunil clearly loves to speak well of his wife:

> *The wonderful support of my wife cannot be underestimated; it's easy to feel sorry for yourself, give up and withdraw. Her encouragement was God's kindness to me in human form. I had a co-worker who had a car accident and serious back injury at the same time that I had my own injury. His wife left and divorced him during his ordeal and I see the pain and bitterness in his eyes. I have a Proverbs 31 wife!*

### Low impact dates

Next, make time for a date. A date is any time that brings you closer as a couple. Here are some easy low-cost ideas:

* Take ten minutes lying in bed really talking and listening to each other. Shut the door and switch off the TV and the phone.
* Choose and watch a DVD or TV program together.
* Share a special takeaway meal at home.
* Rest and cuddle quietly.
* Play cards, or get out a board game.
* Pray for each other.
* Write each other love letters and then take time together to read them out.
* Relax together, listening to music. Talk about your favourite bits, or the memories tagged on.
* Have a picnic, taking a packed lunch to another room, the garden or perhaps out in the car somewhere scenic.

✱ Play 'I love you because ...'. Jane says, 'Bill, I love you because ...' adding something true. Bill replies, 'Thank you. Jane, I love you because ...' and so on. Keep going for as long as you can. This game can turn silly, deep, or both in turn. It's good for parent and child, too.

### Take care

Care for your carer by taking his workload seriously. He's entitled to a Carer's Assessment from the Social Work Department. This should trigger a little money and possibly useful things like respite care. Could you wangle a regular day or afternoon off for him?

He will appreciate a 'Plan B' for when (not if) he's ill or needs a holiday. The best plans are laid before the crisis. You could discuss it with relatives, church contacts or friends, privately paid carers or social services. This process shows your partner that you see his needs as important.

Your well spouse will probably be able to do things you can only dream about. If you can take an interest in these activities without expressing jealousy or frustration, he will feel free to have the refreshment he needs. As a bonus, you can be refreshed by hearing tales of his adventures.

## ROMANCE FOR GROWN-UPS

What about expressing love and sexual desire as an ill spouse? Pain, fatigue, mobility problems, loss of libido, loss of confidence or poor self-image can affect anyone's sex life. Add in a spouse's mundane caring responsibilities and the spark can start to dim.

Sex might be the last thing on your mind now you're ill. But it's unlikely that your well husband or wife's sex drive disappeared when yours did. She may find herself in a lonely prison of secret loss and frustration that's truly hard to handle. Loyalty to you may prevent her from sharing her burdens with anyone. One way to show your concern is to ask her if she'd like to discuss her feelings in confidence with a wise friend, counsellor or pastoral worker.

It shrinks the problem if you're specific about what you can't manage right now and why, adding that you regret missing out. Even if you don't mind for yourself, she deserves your concern and sympathy in this area. Breaking the silence releases both parties to team up and consider other ways around the issue. This has to be better than withdrawing sadly in opposite directions.

As things change and move on, you and your spouse may need to grieve your losses to allow fresh air into the situation. Denial adds a huge burden to a fragile and precious part of married life, so it's worth facing the truth. Sexual expression is bound to change and evolve over a long relationship, even without illness.

Sometimes the gains offset the losses in unexpected ways. Sex is like a barometer, showing ups and downs in a marriage. If you grow as a couple during hard times, this love can spill over into deeper intimacy.

**Making a menu**

Let's get creative. Look at sex like a buffet meal, just for a minute. A three course sit-down meal of starter, main course and dessert can get a bit predictable but a buffet offers far more freedom. As a couple you can see what's on the buffet table and then come and go, snack as you pass by or stay and eat till you're stuffed. You can choose what you fancy in any order you please. Sounds like fun to me.

What can a chronically ill person bring to the feast when it comes to sex? A loving sexual relationship covers a lot of ground apart from inserting Tab A into Slot B:

✱ The pleasures of touch, such as massage, hugs, holding hands, a passing pat and so on.

✱ Intimacy, built by taking time together to talk and share, listening with all your heart and telling the truth in love.

✱ Showing love, by offering help, being considerate, kind, friendly, polite and thoughtful, making eye contact, flirting, smiling, making jokes that don't wound, overlooking an offence, offering genuine compliments, giving treats or gifts, writing love notes, remembering important dates and so on.

✶ Showing respect by attending to personal hygiene, trying to make the most of your appearance and attending carefully to your spouse's concerns and point of view.

✶ Giving and sharing physical pleasure, which can mean kissing, holding, foreplay, penetration, intercourse and orgasm.

It takes a long table to hold all these dishes, even if some things are currently off the menu.

Reading the Song of Songs, it's clear that God is interested in intimacy and romance. We also know he sees the end from the beginning. So your current circumstances neither surprise nor daunt him. He is available to hear and answer your cry in this personal area of life.

Established sexual difficulties deserve some extra attention. You could try a course of sex therapy, available via your doctor. The couple remain in charge of the process and their values are taken into account. Your patient organisation may also have useful tips for your particular situation.

## WIN / WIN

Living with illness is a long hard slog. It's easy to feel defeated and give up. Recently, looking around for fresh inspiration, I was struck by the attitude of our local footie fans.

We live right by the Hibs football ground. Whatever the weather, or the odds, the loyal Hibs fans turn up to support their team. They cheer and boo enthusiastically throughout the match and celebrate with singing far into the night. This is a tribe who relish the fight, regardless of results. It's a good way to live.

May I present the Hibs guide to positive thinking:

✶ As I run out onto the pitch, I'm winning
✶ If I fail and then try again, I'm winning
✶ If I fail a bit and win a bit, it's a draw – and a draw counts for points that boost me up the league, so I'm winning
✶ If I break the rules and come to the ref in repentance, I'm winning

* Losing this time doesn't mean I won't win next time
* All wins should be celebrated by jumping around, hugging complete strangers and roaring approval
* Win or lose, singing and worshipping will focus my mind on previous glories and future victories

## *For reflection*

**1** Is there a bear in your bed?

**2** Choose and try out a low impact date from the list this week.

**3** Dig out your wedding photos and talk about the day. What were the best bits?

*By all means, marry. If you get a good wife, you'll become happy; if you get a bad one, you'll become a philosopher.*

SOCRATES

*If I get married, I want to be very married.*

AUDREY HEPBURN

*To keep your marriage brimming*
*With love in the wedding cup,*
*Whenever you're wrong, admit it,*
*Whenever you're right, shut up!*

OGDEN NASH

# WHAT ABOUT THE KIDS?

One morning long ago, I was in bed, my husband at work and my little girl at school. Presently my three-year-old son came to my bedside, holding a brightly coloured box. 'Can you play this game with me, Mummy?' he asked. Only God knows what it cost me to reply, 'Sorry, sweetheart, Mummy's not well enough to get up and play with you.' As he walked away without a word, my tears flowed once again.

Parenting is a privilege and a joy, but there's no built-in sick leave. It's important, demanding and urgent. It's painful to see your kids suffer along with you. It's hard to watch your spouse struggle with too many

*"This should be interesting."*

responsibilities. Ill single parents, meanwhile, have Everest to climb every day. A couple who are both ill are in for a long battle, along with their children. What's to be done to lighten the load?

### Think straight

First of all, it's crucial to understand that God has not turned away. Letting fear or resentment grow will wreck a parent's peace of mind and warp their vital relationship with God.

The Bible is full of God's concern and love for children and parents. Isaiah 40:1–11 describes God's compassion for his people, finally comparing him to a shepherd:

> *He tends his flock like a shepherd:*
> *he gathers the lambs in his arms*
> *and carries them close to his heart;*
> *he gently leads those that have young.*

ISAIAH 40:11

We can depend on the word of God. This promise has proved its worth in my family over the years. Another useful passage for sick parents is Matthew 18:1–10. Jesus teaches his disciples that they must become like little children to enter the kingdom of heaven. He concludes:

> *See to it that you do not look down on one of these little ones.*
> *For I tell you that their angels in heaven always see the face of*
> *my Father in heaven.*

MATTHEW 18:10 (NIV: 1984)

Jesus reveals the inner workings of heaven, where guardian angels petition the Father. The Father allows the angels of children to skip the queue because he values children highly. He's watching over them day and night. This doesn't mean a pain-free life, because we live in a broken world. It means God never takes his loving eye off the kids. He's always watching over them to bless them.

## Play to your strengths

Let's start with what you've got. You're ill, but you have resources that only you can offer your child. Perhaps you can't do it all, but you can still do something.

First off, children need to feel welcome. A regular time set aside to listen to a child gives him real security and helps to compensate for losses elsewhere. Little ones can be scooped up into Daddy's bed to talk about their day. Bigger children appreciate a comfy spot in the bedroom where they can relax and chat. Toddler bath time offers easy time together, with the adult sitting in a chair or lying on the bath mat. Setting a timer is a good way to show a small child that 'Daddy time' is over for today.

Next, speak it out. Tell your child you love him. Explain some of what's happening and why, even if things are bleak. This stops him worrying that activities have been withdrawn as punishment, or that he has made Mummy ill. Under-fives connect the whole world to themselves and so may react to change with fear or guilt. Older kids may overhear and misunderstand adult conversations. Any child will pick up on a strange or tense atmosphere. If you talk to them directly, you get to choose how to explain issues in a way they can grasp.

Mentally ill parents may find it easier to get moving with their kids rather than getting into tiring conversations. A group activity such as football or swimming is less intense while still offering the child a sense of time spent with love.

Simple touch also communicates love. If you're sore, think about a way to hold or touch your child that won't be so painful. It's good to explain why climbing all over you isn't a good idea today.

Here are some ideas for praying for your child:

* Deal with feelings of guilt and condemnation promptly, knowing that God sees your heart attitude rather than your activity levels.

* Thank God for the gift of your family and that he knew this season of illness would come. He's been preparing you for this task.

* Ask God to pick up the load and parent your children when your energy falls short

* Bring all your concerns about your child to God and let him carry the load.

* Ask God to show you how best to serve and lead your child with what you have available.

* Pray over your child's emotional and spiritual needs, asking specifically for help with obvious issues. Offer your parenting to God and ask him to multiply it to meet your family's needs, like Jesus feeding the five thousand. (Mark 6:30–40)

## BE REASONABLE

It doesn't help to try to reach previous standards in cookery, housekeeping, activities or outings. Things have changed. Children are flexible by nature, since the whole world is new to them. I remain deeply moved by the way my small children accepted me just as I was, a newly sick and incapable mum.

Parenting has become a perfectionist pursuit, with plenty of magazine articles telling us to reach higher and friends who seem to have it all together. What a pity, both for frazzled parents and their bemused 'designer' children. How about aiming for Good Enough Parenting? Do what's needed and draw the line, letting everybody relax along the way.

For example, putting the children ahead of the housework is good use of scarce energy, and visitors who disagree can be politely invited to help out – that'll sort 'em! Genuine helpers, meanwhile, are assets to be treasured and thanked. Granny, Auntie or a friend can ease things along, but don't expect mind reading. Parents can help by explaining what's most needed. A well helper could perhaps come on a family holiday. Good cooks can make food to ease the load.

If your spouse is flat out, regular appreciation of their work helps to prevent resentment. Their priorities will usually differ from yours, but does it really matter?

Children can learn to help at an early age, starting with tidying their toys at bedtime and moving on to simple cleaning, fetching things and helping the cook. So long as they aren't overburdened and their efforts

---

[16] Contact your Social Work Department.

are praised, this is good for their self-esteem. This is one area where your children can outstrip their friends in learning to be practical, helpful, thoughtful and kind.

The dark side of this is the overburdened child carer who comes under massive pressure emotionally and practically, often missing school and lacking a social life. Child carers are now entitled to a carer's assessment[16] and this process is likely to yield extra help and support for child and parent.

Teenagers are naturally immature, experimental and moody. On top of this, some teens react to illness in the family by rebelling, or becoming over-responsible and compliant. It's hard to tell what causes what; perhaps it doesn't help to try.

*"OK, if you're happy with the terms and conditions as outlined in the Sleepover Contract, just scribble your name at the bottom with the blue crayon."*

At times, I found myself reaching for over-high standards with my teenagers. I suspect I was trying to prove that my illness hadn't affected them. With hindsight, this was a really bad idea all round. I'm surprised the poor kids turned out so delightful.

### TLC and PLC

TLC stands for Tender Loving Care. PLC stands for Parental Low Cunning, and both are essential household tools. It's possible, with careful planning, to give your little treasures some fun without killing yourself en route.

For example, we put the sleep back into sleepover in the early years. Any child wishing to sleep over was welcomed but pre-warned that they were expected to go to sleep at a stated hour. If they didn't settle, the resident child would be removed to our bedroom, leaving the visitor to sleep alone. I never had to follow through on this dire threat. As a bonus, other parents appreciated having a post-sleepover child who wasn't wrecked.

Later, teenage parties loomed. We either sent me on a sleepover, leaving my well husband to referee, or changed the start time to noon. Even the most dedicated revellers are ready for bed by midnight after twelve hours of partying. It's easy to keep an eye on proceedings and it's gentler on the neighbours.

It's satisfying to apply your mind to a regular glitch in family life and find a solution. Maybe your children have good ideas, too.

## BUILT ON THE ROCK

*'Therefore everyone who hears these words of mine and puts them into practice is like a wise man who built his house on the rock. The rain came down, the streams rose, and the winds blew and beat against that house; yet it did not fall, because it had its foundation on the rock. But everyone who hears these words of mine and does not put them into practice is like a foolish man who built his house on sand. The rain came down, the streams rose, and the winds blew and beat against that house, and it fell with a great crash.'*

MATTHEW 7:24–27

What does it mean to build your family on a rock, and is it ever too late to start?

A building project begins with a site survey, looking at strengths and weaknesses from all viewpoints. For families, this involves talking honestly to every member, praying over issues and seeing what comes up. Then the foundations are dug and laid, adding strength and removing obstacles that will weaken the structure later on. According to the passage, this crucial step means allowing the Word to penetrate deeply into daily life. This strong foundation will be what saves the building in a storm, so it's worth taking the time and effort to create and maintain it. This means reading child-friendly Bible stories and praying regularly with your children, helping everyone to memorise Bible verses and applying the principles to family life. The house itself, the family, is built by offering respect, fun and compassion for everyone and organising helpful, healthy routines and habits.

Starting well is helpful but it's never too late to welcome God into your family, with or without the support of every member. An ill parent can upbuild and transform their household by praying, planning and making a difference in small ways.

## *For reflection*

**1** Think about the last week with your children. Any highs or lows that come to mind?

**2** Do your children have someone to talk to about the pressures they face? Is there someone you could ask to help in this way?

**3** Lighten a young child's burden with this verse:

*Cast all your anxiety upon him because he cares for you.*

1 PETER 5:7

To do this, cuddle up. Ask gently how he feels about the changes your illness has brought. Take it step by step, repeating the question to see what surfaces. Each difficult feeling can be put into an imaginary shopping trolley as you go. When it's full it can be pushed off an imaginary cliff, with satisfying sound effects. The word 'cast' means throw, so this is applying the meaning at a child's level. Follow up with a brief prayer of thanksgiving and an assurance that God sees and cares.

*Illness is the night side of life, a more onerous citizenship. Everyone who is born holds dual citizenship, in the kingdom of the well and in the kingdom of the sick. Although we all prefer to use the good passport, sooner or later each of us is obliged, at least for a spell, to identify ourselves as citizens of that other place.*

SUSAN SONTAG

*Obstacles are those frightful things you see when you take your eyes off your goals.*

HENRY FORD

*Every child comes with the message that God is not yet discouraged of humanity.*

RABINRANATH TAGORE

# SPIRITUAL FITNESS

## 19

As I travel the illness road, multiple pressures pile on to my spiritual life. At the same time, many previously helpful activities are out of reach. This double whammy leaves me struggling to hang on to God through the pain. I'm not a spiritual giant, or even middle sized – but I've thought a lot about this struggle. I'd like to share some simple, road-tested ways to maintain a healthy spiritual life.

## WORSHIP FOR WEAKLINGS

I hit a major relapse some years ago. I went abruptly from singing in the worship group to lying flat on a pew, unable even to find breath to sing along. As time went by, I realised that my treasured season of service in the worship group was over. I feel the loss to this day. Over the painful months that followed, I learned some life changing lessons about true worship.

Worship is about God, surely? It's about putting him first, focussing on him and clearing space from other pursuits and concerns to consider his beauty. It isn't about how I feel, where I am or what I do with my body. As a New Covenant follower of Jesus, I'm free to do these radical things:

* ✹ come to the throne of God
* ✹ worship in spirit and in truth
* ✹ offer my life as a sacrifice
* ✹ worship with thanksgiving and awe[17]

Gathering with others, singing, standing, kneeling, dancing, clapping and shouting are biblical ways to express this heart attitude. But they are not the core of worship. In fact I think my enjoyment of the music had become

---

[17] See Hebrews 10:19–22, John 4:21–24, Romans 12:1, Hebrews 12:28–29.

a distraction to me. As my singing voice and clapping hands gave way to reclining silently in a corner, I had to learn this the hard way. I can now confidently worship God without moving a muscle, if that is all I have to offer. Like King David, I can bow in worship in my bed. (1 Kings 1:47)

### Toe dance

So as an individual, I'm free to worship God. But can I truly join in worship with others, or must I remain a spectator?

During one Sunday service as I quietly wept with frustration, God reminded me that the hand has four fingers and a thumb. A thumb works with the fingers to grasp, manipulate and carry. It faces the other way

*"I'm sorry madam, could you stop moving your toes. This isn't a happy-clappy church."*

and looks different from the four fingers, all neatly lined up in a row. But without a thumb, the hand can't work properly. I saw that I was a thumb in the Body of Christ, with a different but important part to play.

So I started again with fresh vision, learning to worship in new ways. I learned to mouth or whisper the words of the songs in unison with other singing worshippers. This allowed me to express our shared vision. Joint pain and fatigue put paid to raising my hands, but I could always choose to offer my imperfect heart and my broken body to God. I no longer feel left out as others sing; I am right there worshipping with them. My worship speciality is the Emily Toe Dance, which I invite you to enjoy in any setting. To toe dance, point your toes gently to left and right in time with the music. Smile and rejoice!

The book of Isaiah describes the blessings given to King Cyrus, a man unknowingly called by God for heavenly purposes. I love this particular promise:

> *I will give you the treasures of darkness, riches stored in secret places, so that you may know that I am the LORD, the God of Israel, who summons you by name.*

ISAIAH 45:3 (NIV: 1984)

The sick miss out on ordinary opportunities like joining freely in worship with other Christians. On the other hand, we have the chance to seek out treasure in dark places, like miners digging underground. The things I learned through this difficult time are still sustaining me years later. I regret the need for pain and struggle but I'm deeply grateful for those rich moments of insight. Your issue may not be with singing or worship, but I believe that God is waiting to teach you something new and special through your trials.

## SING A NEW SONG

*Sing joyfully to the Lord, you righteous;*
*it is fitting for the upright to praise him.*

*Praise the Lord with the harp;*
   *make music to him on the ten-stringed lyre.*
*Sing to him a new song;*
   *play skilfully, and shout for joy.*

PSALM 33:1–3

The Bible is full of people bursting into song. Miriam sang for joy when the people of Israel were saved from the Egyptian army.[18] Mary the mother of Jesus sang to God about her pregnancy.[19] The Psalms are outpourings of joy, serenity, triumph, grief, anger, frustration, pain and faith.

These songs are much more than music. They're important records of people meeting with God. Biblical prayer-songs are personal, up-to-date and honest. I found new intimacy with God when I learned to worship in this way.

I'm not talking about literal freshly written songs, although if you're creative in that way, that's wonderful. Many of our finest hymns and songs were written by people living through tough times – you might just create a classic.

Offering a new song means welcoming God into your day. Tell God everything that's on your mind, simply, like a child, and remind him and yourself of his promises. This is your song.

### Why should I?

Sometimes it's hard to face what's on my mind, or to turn my thoughts to God. I'm encouraged by this promise from the book of James;

> *If any of you lacks wisdom, you should ask God, who gives generously to all without finding fault, and it will be given to you.*

JAMES 1:5

As I bring my muddles and failures to God and reflect on his greatness, he can start to instruct, equip, support, heal and comfort me. Along the way I stand to learn a lot about my true self and his true self. If I miss this, I miss out.

---

[18] Exodus 15:19–21.
[19] Luke 1:46–55

Our broken offerings are an acceptable sacrifice to God. Any old Christian can say she loves God when things are going fine, but how many others are in my exact situation today? Nobody. I'm the only one who can offer my song. God is waiting to receive my unique sacrifice. That's a high calling.

## SIN – WHO'S WATCHING?

Some sick people live out their faith unseen, or rarely seen, by anybody else. What's the point of having high standards of integrity? Nobody's there to be inspired.

Well, here's some bracing news; there are at least four viewpoints to consider.

First of all, God sees our hearts as well as our actions. So a sick believer can bring a fragrant and acceptable offering; a precious gift, just for God's pleasure.

Next, *I* see and know the choices I make. I'll build tomorrow on the choices of today. If I win battles here, I can also win healthy self-respect.

Thirdly, we've all met people who made a big impression on us. They spoke, chose, wrote or behaved well and we watched, learned and remembered. In turn, we have the chance to make an impact on others. We may have little opportunity to meet others now, but remember Joseph going from prison to meet Pharaoh? You never know what's around the corner, or who might come your way.

This idea of influencing others is found in Hebrews 11, which describes the lives of Abel, Noah and other heroes of the faith, both well known and unknown. Hebrews 12 tells us we can grow by observing their example:

> *Therefore, since we are surrounded by such a great cloud of witnesses, let us throw off everything that hinders and the sin that so easily entangles. And let us run with perseverance the race marked out for us, fixing our eyes on Jesus, the pioneer and perfecter of our faith.*

HEBREWS 12:1–2

The writer encourages us to do our very best to live like heroes, looking to Jesus as our finest example. We can make choices that honour God, even in the hardest of times. What we learn along the way could be a lifeline to offer someone later on. If we keep at it, according to this verse, Jesus will lead us closer to maturity.

Finally, the devil is also watching, carefully trailing temptation in your path and hoping to see you take the bait. Don't you want to give him a really bad day?

## TRANSFERABLE SKILLS

In a previous book I looked at transferable skills learned by carers.[20] The principle works well for us too. Even when it looks like nothing's happening, we're acquiring useful skills. Here are some good things a sick person might learn during times of ill health:

* Patience
* Problem solving skills
* Creativity
* Perseverance
* Courage
* Endurance
* Sense of humour
* Budget management
* Teamwork
* Trust
* Receiving graciously

* Expertise in your condition and its management
* Acceptance of the frailties of others
* Flexibility
* Realism about your limits
* Good pacing strategies
* Forgiveness
* Humility
* Submission to God's plan
* Self-discipline

Perhaps you feel that the cost of acquiring these skills isn't worth the result, because you won't get a chance to apply them elsewhere. Or you may be facing an uncertain life span, beyond realistic hope of recovery. Let me show you how these skills will come in useful, on Earth and in Heaven.

---

[20] A time to care; loving your elderly parents, pub. IVP

## Shine a light

First, Jesus taught us to use our earthly lives to display the glory of God:

> 'You are the light of the world. A town built on a hill cannot be
> hidden. Neither do people light a lamp and put it under a bowl.
> Instead they put it on its stand, and it gives light to everyone in
> the house. In the same way, let your light shine before others,
> that they may see your good deeds and glorify your Father in
> heaven.'

MATTHEW 5:14–16

Your life is lived before loved ones or professional caregivers. As ordinary living falls away, your source of strength is clearly revealed. I'm not asking the very ill to reach for a higher standard here. I'm saying that your life still counts. You can shine your light even in at times of great weakness. Small moments can speak loudly, challenging and changing others even after you've gone.

This ministry isn't just for those who're dying. I've met many inspirational people who've helped me enormously by their honesty, faith, humour and humility. Some of these people never knew the impact they had on me. Perhaps our meeting was very brief, or I read or heard their words along the way.

Faithful, loving witness to others who are sick is another way to shine your light. Your voice speaks clearly where the voices of the well cannot reach.

## Perfectly useful

Next, we're all going to die one day. In Heaven a new life begins, free from bodily weakness and the endless battle with sin. We'll have new bodies, new freedoms and new, useful jobs to do.

According to Scripture, faithful believers will be given their own responsible role, ruling and administering the earth under God's command. We all need to be prepared for such high level jobs and the training school is here and now. Lessons learned in difficult times will be used in ways we can't imagine now.

If you feel your skills are overlooked by others or swamped by your illness, remember this: every believer will be useful in Heaven. I cling to this on days when I can't get anything done, or even think straight. The best is definitely yet to come – a meaningful, satisfying career in the City of God.

## *For reflection*

**1** Think of a high point in your spiritual life. What led up to it? What did you learn?

**2** What do you think about the idea of singing a new song?

**3** Have a look at the list of transferable skills. Have you got anything to add?

*See, that's nothing but blues, that's all I'm singing about. It's today's blues.*

JIMI HENDRIX

*Earth's crammed with heaven . . . but only he who sees, takes off his shoes.*

ELIZABETH BARRETT BROWNING

*Know pain; know gain.*

INTERESTING ADVERT FOR MY LOCAL
PHYSIOTHERAPIST

# WHAT ABOUT CHURCH?

One winter evening, we arrived at church in time for the pre-service prayer meeting. Sadly, the lift refused to open its doors. My husband climbed the stairs to alert the stewards, leaving me chilling out in the unheated lobby.

Presently he returned to keep me company. Sounds of amateur lift repair floated distantly down the lift shaft. Every breath was visible as a white plume in the frosty air, so we did up our coats again and reached for the gloves. As we waited, we decided to start an alternative prayer meeting. We read the Bible, prayed for each one taking part in the service and asked God nicely if the lift could be fixed before we froze solid. Even my wheelchair was shivering.

I began to wonder if I would get to church at all. Should I ring for a taxi and go home to allow my husband to go on in? The enthusiasm of the stewards was heart-warming but the rest of me was heading for frostbite. Frustration and anger lurked close by. I felt painfully left out in the cold.

As we prayed I looked at Psalm 26, in which King David asks God to uphold him and to test his heart and mind. I realised that my attitudes were being tested too. Reading on, I agreed with David's love for God's house and considered the blessing of meeting together. I had to smile over the closing verse:

> My feet stand on level ground;
> in the great congregation I will praise the Lord.

PSALM 26:12

Now that sounds promising, eh?

After twenty-five minutes, the lift was fixed and up we went. Psalm 26 proved to be very relevant to the evening's theme, we thawed out nicely and it all ended well.

This incident sticks in my mind because it's like my life. I often have to take the long way round but I still have choices. I can choose to stay

positive or allow despair and frustration to rule the moment. This choice
has helped me handle the ups and downs of church membership in a long
season of illness.

## CHURCH, WHAT CHURCH?

Sunil found that his church tried hard to help him continue in his role
after a back injury. He had a lot of adjusting to do, too:

*I was playing bass and acoustic guitar before my injury. I was a worship leader, which meant lots of standing. Once my back was injured I could hardly sit, let alone stand, so my worship leading days were over. I wanted to just give up on music because of the pain. I couldn't even carry my guitar to practice, so my wife had to carry it for me; that too was discouraging. But I persisted anyway through much pain and continued as a guitar player in our church band. They actually moved a chair into the sanctuary for me, with armrests, so I was able to keep playing. After a while I learned to rest and ice up my back before and after playing. Learning my limitations and accepting them took a while. After I moved fully into the acceptance phase, I changed to playing electric lead guitar.*

How's it going with you at church? While some ill people are welcomed and integrated, others find themselves out on a limb. Then some aren't well enough to get there and sit through a service. Access, hearing and seating issues can be a barrier, particularly with older buildings.

Perhaps we expect too much sometimes. But I hear stories of disappointment and frustration from many ill people. How can I give what I have without becoming exhausted? How can I join with the Body of Christ in serving our Master? How can I help the congregation understand what I'm facing?

It can be a lonely struggle for an ill believer. Sometimes I've guiltily wondered if it's worth the effort. And am I still part of the Body if church attendance is not possible at all?

In this chapter we'll look at making the most of a church connection and surviving the lean times.

## FIRST THINGS FIRST

It's painful to feel overlooked or misunderstood by members of your church. Mentally ill believers in particular can find themselves invisible, or maybe you just stopped hearing from anyone after weeks of absence.

If this is you, are you sure you know what's going on, and why? As we've seen, people may feel threatened by your illness, be scared to say the wrong thing, or miss your previous role in their lives. They may think you've backslidden, or you're in a huff with them. If it's hard for you to understand your illness, it's much harder for them.

If only a few stick with you, it's easy to think, 'Well, my church is rubbish, but those two or three friends are fine.' Hang on, though; those two or three are part of the church, the part that's supporting you.

Two active strategies make church life easier; informing and forgiving. First, speak up. Start small; try to explain some things, once in a while. If someone gets the idea, ask them to spread the word. Be specific:

* I can't come to the Bible study because of the stairs
* I'll be in hospital for four weeks from next Friday and would welcome visitors
* I'm finding the social side of things hard work, please look out for me

Try a simple request. If it would help to have a visitor who comes to listen and pray with you, a lift on a Sunday or help with cooking or shopping, ask your church leader to look into it. Don't wait sadly for people to guess.

Next, I've learned the hard way to practice forgiveness *every time* I feel the need. This one is a stretch because I feel that Christians should know better. Forgiveness doesn't mean they're right, or I'm right for that matter. It means I've decided to turn away from resentment and hurt. It allows genuine contact to continue through hard times and makes room for the Holy Spirit to move in the situation. Once I feel a bit better, it's easier to resolve the problem. If I can't resolve it, I have to go on forgiving regardless. In the end, I may need to take myself out of an unsustainable situation. Even then, I have to forgive on my way out the door.

## I CAN'T GO TO CHURCH

Another pitfall for the sick believer is not getting to church at all, or so rarely that there's not much of a connection. This means learning how

*"Mary and I noticed that you hadn't been to church for a while.
We're just checking that you're still a Christian?"*

to grow in God with little outside input, which came as a shock for me. I was used to sound preaching, wise pastoral advice, good fellowship and inspiring music. Like many a missionary before me, I had to learn to live without such luxuries.

I believe in the value of active church membership. It needs to be a high priority for every follower of Jesus. We need others and they need us. Even so, let's not throw out the baby with the bathwater. We belong to God forever and he loves us forever. He's still active in our lives, ready to help us to grow and be fruitful. We may be out on the edge of the local church but we're still part of Christ's Body and included in God's plans.

### Church is a verb

I have a personal responsibility to follow God and love others, even if I feel my own needs are overlooked. If I'm not well enough to go to church, I can still do church. Here are some pick'n'mix strategies to be tried out as energy allows:

* I'll intercede for others, or phone someone to ask for prayer for my own needs
* I'll e-mail my Christian friend in another city
* I'll send a card to a bereaved neighbour
* I'll find a smile for my carer
* I'll ask God to give me an opportunity to share my faith
* I'll serve others through an Internet group for people with my condition
* I'll ask the minister to bring communion to me
* I'll listen attentively to some Christian music
* I'll read my Bible and add in a good devotional aid
* I'll look into joining a social network site to keep in touch with others
* I'll pray my way through the church directory, name by name, day by day
* I'll read up on world missions, pray, and make a small donation
* I'll explore online church services and other teaching resources
* I'll ask about hosting a one-off prayer gathering or small group in my home
* I'll ring a friend from church to catch up on the news
* I'll write to my minister to explain why I'm not at services and to reassure him that I still view myself as a member

In quietly doing these things, I live out my faith with and for others. I'm doing church in bite-sized chunks instead of in a Sunday morning session. The Body of Christ is the local and global church but also any Christian that God sends my way. My version of meaningful fellowship is spread over several countries.

### A silver lining

It's hard when regular church attendance is derailed but over time I discovered hidden benefits. For one thing, I had become a bit blasé about going to church. These days, when I arrive at a service I'm delighted to be there. I'm ready to go, entering in, listening with all my attention and eager to mix with others. The less I have, the more I appreciate it.

Also, it's possible for members of a lively church to live off the group's spirituality and vision. I went from service to service without ever realising that I'd become passive. Once that was withdrawn, I had to choose. I could either give up or wake up. There's no fence to sit on any more.

I was used to seeking wise advice for every difficulty. Alone at home, I was forced into learning to hear directly from God. I grew up, taking responsibility for myself and my spiritual life. Perhaps it would never have happened without the pain of illness and isolation.

Ministry is much more than what happens in a church building on a Sunday. Your love for God may drive you to serve your community in a way that suits your limits. Now the Kingdom of God is moving outside the four walls. This can only be a good thing.

Of course it helps enormously if your congregation reaches out to you. I think each ill person in membership deserves an informal advocate, like a missionary representative. Maybe there's someone you could approach about this.

## I'VE HAD ENOUGH

The sick sometimes feel that their church is not meeting their needs, which tend to increase as attendance decreases. This may be true. If so, it might be worth taking the initiative to discuss some specific issues with appropriate people. But beware of blaming your church for your own difficulties.

For example, Bill loves to be fully involved with church life. Now he's ill, he often misses meetings, he's dropped off rotas and he feels left out. He's angry, hurt and thinking about leaving. The trouble is, Bill has a blind spot. He's overlooking the part played by his new limits. So he's expecting his church activities and relationships to stay as they were.

Here's an action plan for Bill, to help him update his church connection:

* Face his limits and grieve over his losses in this area
* Give thanks for past joys and commit to serving God in future
* Choose forgiveness, to let healing flow over his hurt feelings
* Think through and adjust the way he serves and connects to his church
* Honestly approach others to explain his situation and ask for help
* Consider talking to a trusted third party, to ease his mind and get a fresh viewpoint

Not easy, is it? But after working through the plan, Bill's better placed to decide if a move would really do the trick. After all, his congregation may need him to teach them how to handle a sick believer.

### Leaving and arriving

If a move is really, truly the best and only option, it's worth the effort to leave well. This means explaining the problem, if at all possible. Then it's about saying goodbye graciously rather than disappearing without trace. This frees you and others to grow and move on.

It also helps to arrive well, to approach the new minister to explain your situation and make a real effort to talk to new people. It can be a relief to have a fresh start, free of the expectations and patterns of the past. It's a good opportunity to reassess what you currently have to give to a church.

Moving church is always a serious business and can be quite traumatic. Many Christians carry their hurts with them into other churches. Then they find themselves facing and reproducing the old problems in a new setting. So it's worth the effort of praying through any difficulties during and after a move.

## NEVER ALONE

*And we know that in all things God works for the good of those who love him, who have been called according to his purpose... If God is for us, who can be against us?... Who shall*

*separate us from the love of Christ? Shall trouble or hardship or
persecution or famine or nakedness or danger or sword?*

ROMANS 8:28, 31b, 35

This famous passage offers hope for all, including those who feel
wounded by the church. Paul's starting point is purpose. God remains
actively involved in every situation and completely committed to us,
now and in future. We're destined to become like Jesus, mature, gracious
and useful to God. Our position as redeemed believers is solid, built to
last. No disaster or trial can come between us and the loving purposes of
our God.

He has not forgotten me and wants to use me even now. I can rely on
him to meet my needs and to speak words of life over me.

## *For reflection*

**1** Think about the last few months. Write down a few church related
difficulties and blessings. Offer the tricky bits up to God and ask him
to reveal treasure from the dark places, according to the promise in
Isaiah 45:3.

**2** Are there ideas from the list under 'Church is a verb' that you could
try out?

**3** Look again at Bill's experiences in the 'I've had enough' section. Are
you struggling with church relationship issues? Try one step from the
action plan to see what happens.

**4** Read the full passage in Romans 8:23–35, aloud if you wish. Allow the
encouraging truth to filter down into today's challenges.

*Really I feel less keen about the Army every day. I think the
Church would suit me better*

WINSTON CHURCHILL

*The responsibility of tolerance lies with those who have the wider vision.*

GEORGE ELIOT

*The church is not a gallery for the better exhibition of eminent Christians, but a school for the education of imperfect ones.*

HENRY WARD BEECHER

# HOW TO SURVIVE YOUR OWN DEATH 21

Terminal illness is life's last big challenge. In this chapter we'll explore the pressures on a dying person and the people that love him, and look at ways to finish the race well.

## ETERNITY STARTS NOW

What's the difference between life and death? Jesus taught that eternal life begins at the point of sincere belief:

> *I tell you very truly, whoever hears my word and believes him who sent me has eternal life and will not be judged but has crossed over from death to life.*

JOHN 5:24

A person can be transformed by receiving the gift of eternal life. Looking at it from this angle, the biggest change comes at salvation, not at death. Bodily death is not the end of a Christian's life. Eternal, spiritual life persists unchanged within.

### What is death?

* Death is a natural part of life in a fallen world. It's not a failure or a mistake.
* Dying is a huge transition. As loved ones start to grieve over losing you, you must grieve the loss of everything you've known in this world.
* Death is a mystery. You only die once, so nobody can tell you how it really feels.

It's comforting to know that Jesus has personally experienced and defeated death. He can be relied on to understand our struggles as we go through the last season of life.

## NEW CHALLENGES, FAMILIAR ISSUES

The prospect of death is a new challenge for those who've adjusted to illness. Still, it's not entirely new; it's more like the last lap in a long race.

Joel's cancer has returned and this time it can't be cured. As he gets sicker, he realises that his time is short. Once again, Joel rounds the familiar corner and runs through feelings of loss, grief and shock. His 'Why?' questions resurface. Once again, Joel's friends and family must face their own pain.

### Out of synch

On top of all this, Joel is trying to discern God's will for his future. Is it healing – or heaven? He finds himself bouncing from faith to fear, acceptance to battle and denial to despair. This is the Christian's version of the normal psychological reaction to loss. It's the stage of bargaining, exploring different ways to avoid unwanted change. It's deeply uncomfortable but it's not a failure of faith.

Joel's loved ones are also switching painfully from viewpoint to viewpoint. There are inevitably times when they don't all see eye to eye. Again, this isn't a failure; it's a normal reaction to love and loss.

So today, Joel's able to see the future clearly and his daughter Megan is in denial. He could try simply acknowledging the way she feels and then leave the topic for another day. Perhaps tomorrow will offer a better match in attitudes. He could graciously offer Megan the space to be imperfect, just not coping very well for a bit. Maybe he could offer himself the same grace too.

Denial is a defence mechanism, so there's no point taking it away from Megan without anything to replace it. A trusted person could help Megan work towards accepting reality. This will help her now and after

Joel's death. Time away from caring for Joel will also relieve the pressure, if possible.[21]

## Unfinished business

Terminally ill people often feel bad about tasks left undone, relationships gone sour or unfinished plans. As you look back over your life, it's only fair to note the good things too. See if you can spot God's provision over the years; it's often hidden at the time. Thanksgiving moves the spotlight from personal failings onto God's perfection.

Here are some practical ideas:

* Is there anything you can do to resolve a relationship? For example, ask for or offer forgiveness, explain something or repay a debt. Of course, it takes two; but you could maybe try from your end and leave the rest with God.

* For unfulfilled plans, could you share money, vision, strategy or encouragement with others working in that area? It's okay just to do what you can, within your tight limits. God sees your heart. Try to share generously without strings. Remember that others are given their own calling and responsibility before God.

* Take time to do business with God, laying down with humility what can't be fixed or completed.

* Ask God for forgiveness. The cross still stands; you can be released right now. Forgive yourself as you forgive others.

## Be yourself

Some people avoid terminal illness as if it's catching, which is hurtful. But even those who visit may expect to see you healed, or calm and full of faith. Visitors may hold you in reverence or try to jolly you along. This is a heavy burden if you're sore, uncomfortable, embarrassed, angry, irritable or scared.

---

[21] The MacMillan charity has trained nurses to support anybody affected by terminal illness. They don't offer hands-on patient care, although they can advise about how to care and where to find respite and home care.

Perhaps it's time to drop the mask. We all fall short of the glory of God. Living and dying perfectly is not an option. Being more open saves energy and allows you to be yourself.

A friend may respond to your struggles with the bracing comment, 'Oh, but you've done so well with this illness!' This is missing the point. Dying is a brand new challenge. He may not get it, but that doesn't make you a bad person. Or him, for that matter.

It's dangerously easy for very ill people to get their own way by manipulating others. Maintaining your integrity shows respect, while offering them the freedom to respond.

## OLD FRIENDS, NEW CHALLENGES

It's a brutal transition for those who love you. The stress can trigger old tensions, or new ones can emerge. On the other hand, rifts can be healed. Sometimes all these things happen within the same family or group.

Relationships change with terminal illness, just as they did after diagnosis. If you have enough energy, good communication really helps. A group e-mail list offers instant news bulletins from you or another.

Someone might go silent on you unexpectedly, driven away by her own grief or fear. You may need to reach out to fix the rift, or let her go ahead of time.

There are other kinds of distance. Lara's brother can't face the pain of her terminal illness. He's withdrawn emotionally while continuing to care for her practically. Lara could try talking to him directly, involving a trusted friend or arranging for him to have more support. If it can't be resolved, she still has choices. She could make the best of it or move, perhaps to another relative's home or into a hospital or hospice. A move sometimes improves overburdened relationships.

Small children naturally connect life events with themselves. They may believe that Daddy is ill because they were naughty. This burden can be lifted by explaining clearly that it isn't their fault.

## I'M SCARED

If you're afraid, shrink it down. What's at the root?

* If it's fear of death, or Hell, you could ask your minister to talk through the basis of your salvation and pray with you.
* If you're afraid of the process of death, or of uncontrolled symptoms, try talking to your doctor or palliative care nurse.
* If you have specific concerns about dying alone, loss of choices or other practicalities, making a death plan allows you to regain some control.
* If you're afraid of what will happen at home after your death, make your will and talk things through. Having a plan is very restful, even if it's not perfect.

Unvoiced feelings hold enormous power, so sharing them is a good idea. Have another look at handling fear in Chapter 10.

## GETTING ORGANISED

Dying naturally sparks fear of the unknown. It's a bit like being pregnant and pondering the birth to come. If mothers-to-be can write a birth plan, why not make a death plan? A good plan helps to give a sense of control and lets everybody knows what you want. A helper could perhaps find things out and write your plan down.

First of all, look for the gaps. If you're living with relatives who have plenty of time to care for you, perhaps you'll want pastoral visits. If you have only one person on hand, your carer will need regular time off. If you live alone, your gap to fill is nursing care and practical support. Perhaps you need to find out what's available locally. It helps to research and plan these things before a crisis hits.

Here are some useful things to put in your death plan:

* Where you'd prefer to spend your last days – at home, hospital, hospice
* Who you do and don't want to see
* Music you might like to hear

✳ Consider making an Advance Directive, a legally binding document to spell out what you want in the way of technical intervention when you're in your last days. Or arrange for someone you trust to take Power of Attorney and make decisions for you if you're not able to do it for yourself. Start soon; the process takes several weeks to complete

✳ Funeral arrangements

✳ Anything else that strikes you as important

This may seem off-putting. But if you don't think about it beforehand, someone else will be left guessing your wishes. Once the plan is ready, discuss it with your carers, give a copy to your doctor and have another copy by your bed in case you're admitted.

## BY HEAVENLY APPOINTMENT

God has a plan for your death and mine. He gives personal attention to every aspect of human life:

> *Precious in the sight of the LORD is the death of his saints.*

PSALM 116:5

The word translated as 'precious' implies lovingly and carefully tended. A trustworthy God watches over us as we cross over into Heaven.

What about the timing? King Solomon applied his wisdom to this question:

> *There is a time for everything,*
>   *and a season for every activity under the heavens:*
>   *a time to be born and a time to die,*
>   *a time to plant and a time to uproot . . .*
> *. . . Since no one knows the future,*
>   *who can tell some else what is to come?*
> *As no one has power over the wind to contain it; so no one has*
> *power over the day of their death.*

ECCLESIASTES 3:1–2 and 8:7–8a

The passage teaches that the God who made us also chose the right day for each one to die. We know from Psalm 116, above, that God travels faithfully alongside the dying. Together these truths build a safe boundary.

In our high-tech health care system, it can be hard to navigate this issue. According to the passage above, man does not have the right to deliberately end a life, even in the face of suffering. But comfort and dignity strike me as far more important than another few days of machine-aided struggle. As life draws to a close, the focus of good treatment changes from cure to care.

If you feel tempted to hasten your own death, or to help a loved one die, please ask for help today. Don't bear this burden alone. You may be suffering from treatable depression, or struggling with worries that could be relieved. If the issue is pain or other symptoms, hospice care or palliative home care can offer you the best chance of getting on top of things. As your illness moves on, medication, services or equipment may need to change. It pays to make sure you have everything that's on offer to fit today's needs.

## WHAT ABOUT HEAVEN?

Heaven can seem a bit theoretical until the chips are down. Now's the time to appreciate how wonderful the next life will be. Here's a taste of what's in store.[22] We can't grasp the full extent now:

> *No eye has seen, no ear has heard, no mind has conceived what God has prepared for those who love him.*

CORINTHIANS 2:9b

As Christian believers, we'll be changed in Heaven:

* We'll have new bodies, free from decay and discomfort, 1 John 3:2 and Rev 7:15–17

---

[22] Chrstians vary in their approach to Millenial theology. Personally, I approach the verses in this section from a simple, expectant perspective; God plans good things for us.

* We'll put sin, shame, grief and pain behind us, both our own and that of others, Rev 21:4
* We'll be permanently filled with joy and pleasure, Psalm 16:11
* We'll be with Jesus, with no guilt or sin to check our intimacy, Luke 23:43

We'll have exciting things to do:

* We're invited to the great wedding and we'll marry our Bridegroom, Rev 19:6–9
* We'll serve God in meaningful ways, Rev 22:3, 5
* We'll have loving relationships that are free of sin and shame, 1 Cor 13:12 and Rev 7:9
* We'll inherit the kingdom prepared for us, Matt 25:34
* We'll live in a community built for us by God, John 14:2–3
* We'll enter the garden of Paradise and eat the fruit of the tree of life, Revelation 2:7
* We'll joyfully worship God in the company of others, Rev 7:9–12
* We'll learn and understand the purposes of God, Ephesians 2:6–7
* We'll be happy forever, in contrast to this short earthly life, 2 Cor 5:1

## LOVE BEYOND DEATH

So Heaven is going to be amazing. But what about the people we love? How will they fare once we're gone?

Remember that God has his own purposes for your special people. He's promised never to leave them. You won't be there to see them recover, start to smile again and realise they've grown – but they will.

Caring for others can continue after death. It's satisfying to know you've done your best for those who remain. Here are some ideas:

* Make or update your will; this makes sure your wishes are followed and saves your family stress and potential hardship
* Nominate someone in your will to take care of your online presence on Facebook and so on, to avoid your picture popping up forever – and tell them the passwords

* Put your will, passport, pension and insurance paperwork, property deeds, birth, marriage or divorce certificates, car and driver documents and any other paperwork together, clearly marked, and tell someone where it is
* Write letters for others to enjoy afterwards. If you have last wishes to share, remember that things will change. Your loved ones need and deserve freedom to find their own way. Their priorities will naturally differ from yours. Last wishes are not a substitute for sorting out your unfinished business!
* For little ones, a memory book with photos and simple accounts of time spent together will be a precious reminder of your love
* Are you the only one who knows where the pipes run under the garden or where the shed keys are kept? Tell someone now, or make a note and put it in with the other paperwork

Pray for those you love; as E. M. Bounds said, 'God shapes the world by prayer. Prayers are deathless. They outlive the lives of those who uttered them.'

### A parting gift

Joseph faced his death at a great age:

> 'Then Joseph said to his brothers, I am about to die. But God will surely come to your aid and take you up out of this land to the land he promised on oath to Abraham, Isaac and Jacob.
> And Joseph made the sons of Israel swear . . . you must carry my bones up from this place.'

GENESIS 50:24-25

Joseph knew that God's plan for the promised land was not yet complete. Joseph had played his part and he trusted God to finish the job. He was so confident that he made his brothers swear to bring his bones along, to rest where he belonged. This shining vision was his parting gift.[23]

You may feel you don't have anything impressive to pass along. But the Bible teaches over and over that God will bless a believer's descendants;

---

[23] See Exodus 13:19 for what happened to Joseph's bones

*'Understand, therefore, that the Lord your God is indeed God. He is the faithful God who keeps his covenant for a thousand generations and lavishes his unfailing love on those who love him and obey his commands.'*

DEUTERONOMY 7:9

A thousand generations is a lot of people and a long, long time. That's quite an inheritance to leave behind you.

The childless can also leave a blessing. As we do our best to live and love despite life's troubles, others are watching. Think about those who have influenced you for good. Perhaps they never knew how much they helped you. Each one of us can ask God to use our imperfect lives to bless and teach others. This is our lasting legacy.

## *For reflection*

**1** What's the biggest challenge you face right now?

**2** Are you finding it hard to agree with the viewpoint of people around you? Could any of you benefit from a listening ear?

**3** Choose one of the points mentioned about Heaven and read the verse attached. Think about how this will change today's situation. Work your way through the list to increase your vision for the next life. What do you think about making a death plan? What would you put into yours?

*If you can't be a good example, be an awful warning.*

ANON

*While I thought that I was learning how to live, I have been learning how to die.*

LEONARDO DA VINCI

*Therefore we do not lose heart. Though outwardly we are wasting away, yet inwardly we are being renewed day by day. For our light and momentary troubles are achieving for us an eternal glory that far outweighs them all. So we fix our eyes not on what is seen, but on what is unseen. For what is seen is temporary, but what is unseen is eternal.*

2 CORINTHIANS 4:16-18

*Here is the test to find whether your mission on earth is finished: if you're alive, it isn't.*

RICHARD BACH

*Now comes the mystery*

THE LAST WORDS OF REV. HENRY WARD BEECHER

# A DIFFERENT GIFT

Many years ago, during a family party, my sister-in-law and I retreated to the kitchen. We cut up a large and splendid birthday cake and laid the slices out attractively on platters to serve to forty guests. Realising that my diabetic father couldn't have cake, I took a small bunch of grapes from a fruit bowl and arranged them on a napkin on a small plate. Taking cake platter in one hand and Dad's plate in the other, I returned to the function room and went first to Dad. I told him I wanted to be sure he had a treat too, gave him his grapes and went on to offer cake to all comers.

This incident came to mind recently as I prayed over the latest illness-related loss in my life. I remember Dad's face lighting up when he realised I'd thought of him, even though he couldn't have cake like the rest of the gang. I sensed God was posing me a question; 'Emily, do you feel deprived because I gave you grapes instead of cake?'

My answer, after careful thought, is 'No'. God has always had me in mind. As I look back over many years of illness, I can see the unbroken thread of God's provision. It never failed, even when the situation was so stressful that his gifts weren't clear to me at the time. It's not as if God gave my neighbour cake and left me hungry. He carefully supplied my needs at the right time with a loving smile. The key is not what I got on my plate but that my Father loves me and thinks of my needs. I'm a daughter, not an orphan.

Now, I'm not smiling serenely like a statue of Buddha, detached from the troubles and temptations of this world. I hate being ill and I long to be well. I hate the endless restrictions on my family, too. I hurt, cry, mope, grump and fret against my limits. But I see that loss and illness is only one side of the coin. On the other side I find love, provision, adventures and unexpected riches. A life with persistent illness is a major challenge but it's not a dead end, as I feared all those years ago.

A final overview of Joseph's story shows me two underlying principles:

* God's plans will come to pass in the life of a person who follows God
* Choosing a good attitude builds strength for the future

These principles really worked for Joseph. He was free to grow and to change his world for good, even though he was denied the freedom to make ordinary life choices.

Joseph's perspective on an extraordinary life is expressed in his loving words to those rascally brothers in Genesis 50:20:

> 'You intended to harm me, but God intended it for good to accomplish what is now being done, the saving of many lives.'

What a hero. I can think of no better companion to inspire me as I live hopefully within the harsh limits of illness.

## FOR REFLECTION

**1** Has God given you grapes instead of cake?

**2** Can you see points of contact between your life experience and Joseph's story?

**3** What do you think of the two principles offered above? Can you think of times when either of them have applied to your own situation?